Corporate Ethics in a Time of Globalization

Klaus M. Leisinger and Karin M. Schmitt

Basel/Colombo, May 2003

Second Edition: 2003
© Klaus M. Leisinger and
    Karin M. Schmitt

ISBN 955-599-333-5

Printed and Published in Sri Lanka
by

VISHVA LEKHA
Printers

41 Lumbini Avenue
Ratmalana Sri Lanka

Contents

Foreword

A sudden flash of a new truth, a fresh reality or the shock of a bitter experience may instantly transform the consciousness of an individual person. Those of us who practice mindfulness meditation for our inner peace also promote and engage in mass meditation practices along with thousands of others in the belief that a critical mass of peace consciousness can be created in the collective consciousness of a community as a whole that will lead to outer peace in the society.

When reading through the book **Corporate Ethics in a Time of Globalization** by Klaus M. Leisinger and Karin M. Schmitt it dawned on me that they are also engaged in a similar but scholarly task of transforming the consciousness of all those who are associated with corporations. I got the feeling that they are initiating an educational process through which they expect to create a critical mass of ethical consciousness in all those stakeholders in the corporate sector both national and multinational.

However, though corporations have acquired rightly or wrongly personhoods, under constitutional laws and judgments with many rights and protections yet they are not human beings. They, of course, are creations of humans. Humans have both a consciousness and a conscience. So creating a critical mass of peace consciousness and a collective peace conscience through mass meditations is a goal that may be achieved. Attempting to create a critical mass of an ethical consciousness in the corporate world is a much harder task. Yet the authors, in my opinion, are attempting to achieve exactly this objective.

This book is about corporate ethics in a time of globalization and not about globalization as such. To my understanding the book is aimed at all those who are associated with corporations. It is like a text book on corporate ethics and excludes nothing relevant to the subject. With the onset of economic globalization corporations wield more power than governments and people.

Hence it is necessary for even the common citizens to know what the corporations are all about and intricacies of their conduct. In a balanced and unbiased manner the authors have tried to broaden and deepen our knowledge on these matters.

As far as the poor and the powerless in the world are concerned the history of corporations reveals how they contributed to perpetrate their suffering. Between 1600 and 1760 the East India Company which was the first to get corporate status from Queen Elizabeth surpassed all others in their pursuit to dominate the rest of the world both economically and politically. Later they spared no pains to get laws passed in England to facilitate them to put their smaller competitors out of business. When the American revolutionaries with the BostonTea Party put the East India Company in its place they hardly would have imagined that another corporate era with more power than ever before would originate from their own free country, extend to others and enslave economically the whole world during the following two centuries. What has come to be known as globalization, which some equate to the new phase of capitalism, is a strategy to bring under a network of corporations all financial interests undermining cultures and livelihoods of the majority of people in the world.

No honest person will accept globalization as a natural process that came about as a consequence of consumers' demand for goods and services. It is a global expression of the self-interest of powerful persons and groups in all departments of business, industrial, financial, political, cultural and other sectors of society whose common value is measured in terms of money. The very fact that, as some scholars have pointed out, that the daily movement of capital in the international markets, exceed several times more than the aggregate of foreign exchange of all states together is enough evidence as to the extent to which the corporations control our lives. While most of this flow of capital is speculative it's only a fraction of the total amount that goes into the economy.

The authors believe that to change this situation revival of ethics in the corporate sector is most important. They strongly maintain that multinational corporations who are the main agents of globalization have to make a constructive contribution towards goals of political stability and humanity. They are of the conviction that it can be done and it has to be done if corporations are to survive.

In the words of the authors:

At least for enlightened companies, corporate success today comprises more than simply the level of quarterly profits. Profit making to a company is what food is to a human being – an absolute necessity. Just as no reasonable person will define his or her purpose in life as exclusively the intake of food, enlightened companies acquire legitimacy for their profit making through their social value-added. The reputation of a company is increasingly becoming one of the most valuable assets, even if it does not appear directly in the balance sheet – but this is likely to change in the very near future in view of the substantial efforts made in the field of social responsibility reporting. The judgment of society which gives justification to a company's reputation depends essentially on whether the company is perceived as contributing to the implementation of social values.

The authors have drawn heavily from the classical philosophers as well as from the wisdom of modern thinkers and scholars. Plenty of current experiences in the corporate sector are cited and critically highlighted, sometimes most ruthlessly, in their prescription for corrective action. They ask "If the moral level of firms in a highly developed industrial nation with its thicket of rules and regulations proves so questionable, what are we to expect of those doing business in developing countries, with their institutional shortcomings and dearth of sound governance ?"

"This book is a must for all those who belong to the business world big or small if they want to pursue their businesses with success as well as with social responsibility. As I mentioned earlier it is a complete text book for them. Nothing is left out - definitions, differences in meanings such as ethics and morality, guidelines from the CEO to all those working in the company, facing up to corruption, harmonizing personal morality with corporate morality, dealing with media and so on.

That is not all. All of us living in a time of globalization can benefit immensely from this book to get an in depth understanding of the business world we live in and make choices as to the roles we should play to stop the destructive tide and enhance the constructive trends."

A. T. Ariyaratne
Sarvodaya Headquarters,
Moratuwa. Sri Lanka.
20th April 2003

PART I

BUSINESS ETHICS: IDEAL AND REALITY

As Paul Streeten once pointed out, a person cannot be objective, pragmatic, and idealistic all at the same time.[1] Analysis of a problem—the diagnosis of a situation as unsatisfactory and in need of improvement—is always influenced by value premises, without which the existing situation cannot even be assessed as deficient. To an even greater extent, any "remedy" proposed requires the acknowledgment of objectives and values to be realized. Not until they have been identified and clarified is it possible to determine the direction in which to seek the solution to existing difficulties.

To make clear the moral concepts and values that the authors recognize, Chapter 1 explains what they understand by morality and ethics, and then relate that understanding to business enterprises. Chapter 2 examines the conflicts that confront companies in countries whose laws, manners, and customs are at odds with our ideas of what is morally right, and discusses the flaws of "ethical relativism." Chapter 3 goes into the expectations that society at large has of business organizations, while Chapter 4 seeks to define corruption so as to be able to form an objective moral judgment on it, and consider the destructive consequences of large-scale corruption. Chapter 5 looks at the perceptions of both the public and managers themselves of the moral quality of corporate conduct. Chapter 6 considers the current state of stakeholder relations in light of all these perceptions and changing demands on corporations. The concluding chapter in Part I examines these issues in light of the recent push toward globalization.

---

1. Paul Streeten, Foreword, in *Das Wertproblem in der Sozialwissenschaft*, 2nd ed., By Gunnar Myrdal (Bonn, Bad Godesberg: Verlag Neue Gesellschaft, 1975), 13.

1. Morality and Ethics

*Morality is not just some desideratum of the weak for
their protection or an instrument of the strong for
tethering the weak, but a factor of utmost importance
for society as a whole and its welfare. Had history
not seen so many sins committed against morality,
humankind would have been spared a surfeit of
suffering.*

Victor Kraft[2]

In everyday speech, the words "morals" and "ethics" are used to mean roughly the same thing, even though they do not. By morals we mean certain norms that govern our behavior—primarily toward our fellow humans, but also with respect to nature and our own persons. The discipline of ethics, on the other hand, is concerned with describing the subject and making comparisons, and it evaluates morality and morals.

Morality passes judgment on human behavior as good or bad. In doing so it pronounces on merit and demerit and is thus value-oriented. But passing judgment on a certain set of facts or circumstances does not suffice to translate morality into action. The essence of morality is that it points out the road to be taken to realization. So it also has to pose demands; these are what give morality its normative character. Norms predicate values—they call for values to be put into effect.

Norms function, however, only to the extent that—and for as long as—they appear self-evident to someone. If we demand something that does not appear self-evident to others, we have to substantiate what is demanded. Controversies over ethics frequently suffer from the fact that the disputants base their moral norms on disparate values. What one party holds to be a value, the other may see as just the opposite. In addition, often no distinction is made between the value judgment and the facts of a case, although sound judgment ought really to presuppose scrupulous clarification of the facts.

Philosophical ethics is of particular importance here because it differs from legal, religious, cultural and personal approaches to ethics by seeking to conduct the study of morality through a rational, secular

---

2.   Victor Kraft, *Die Grundlagen der Erkenntnis und der Moral*, Erfahrung und Denken, Schriften zur Förderung der Beziehungen zwischen Philosophie und Einzelwissenschaften vol. 28 (Berlin: Duncker & Humblot, 1968), 92 f.

outlook that is grounded in notions of human well-being. A major advantage of a philosophical approach to ethics is that it avoids the subjectivity, arbitrariness and irrationality that may characterize cultural or totally personal moral views. It is fundamentally opposed to moralizing, which is the exercise of a type of social pressure to make others behave in a way that one thinks they should.

Generally speaking, there are two traditions in modern philosophical ethics regarding how to determine the ethical character of actions. One argues that actions have no intrinsic ethical character but acquire their moral status from the consequences that flow from them. The other tradition claims that actions are inherently right or wrong. The former is called a *teleological* approach to ethics, the latter, *deontological*.[3]

A teleological outlook is particularly appealing because it takes a pragmatic, common-sense approach to ethics. Simply put, teleological thinkers claim that the moral character of actions depends on the simple, practical matter of the extent to which actions actually help or hurt people. Actions that produce more benefits than harm are "right"; those that don't are "wrong." This outlook is best represented by Utilitarianism, a school of thought originated by the British thinker Jeremy Bentham (1748-1832) and refined by John Stuart Mill (1806-1873).

The difficulty of employing a teleological approach should not be underestimated, however: A full account of an action's results means not only careful analysis of the immediate consequences to all involved and astute discernment of the quality and comparative value of the effects experienced, but an uncovering of the subtle, indirect, farreaching and long-term results as well. An accurate teleological analysis requires great patience, impressive powers of observation and a keen understanding of how people actually respond to various experiences. Nonetheless, this flaw should not overshadow the genuine advantages of a teleological approach to ethics. For the most part, it makes great common sense to link the ethical character of actions or policies to their practical outcome.

The second major tradition in philosophical ethics, the deontological approach, is based on the idea that actions have *intrinsic* moral value. Some actions are considered *inherently good* (truth-telling, keeping promises, respecting the rights of others); others are bad (dishonesty, coercion, theft, manipulation). No matter how much good comes from lying, argues a deontological thinker, the action will never be right.

---

3. See Thomas White, "Ethics," Chapter 1, *Business Ethics: A Philosophical Reader* (New York: Macmillan Publishing, 1993).

Philosophy's most representative deontological thinker is Immanuel Kant (1724-1804). Kant believed that he had discovered the fundamental moral law that would determine the ethical character of an action without regard to its consequences. Kant called his moral law the *categorical imperative*—a command that holds no matter what the circumstances: "Act only according to that maxim by which you can at the same time will that it should become a universal law of nature." He believed further that the validity of this ethical principle stemmed from reason itself and from our nature as free, rational moral agents with inherent value.

Like a teleological approach to ethics, a deontological outlook has much to commend it. Analyzing an ethical dilemma takes on a much narrower focus than when approached teleologically. The only question one has to ask is: Which actions are inherently good? Instead of engaging in complex projections of the primary and secondary consequences of some act, we focus simply on the deed itself. The difficulty with this approach, however, is its inflexibility. If lying is intrinsically wrong, there is no way to justify it even when it produces more good than harm. If we lie in order to help someone, for example, a deontological approach still condemns it. And this total lack of compromise makes a deontological standard a difficult one to live by.

Between teleological and deontological approaches to ethics, then, we see the basic elements that can be used in determining the ethical character of actions. One school of thought points to the results, the other to the actions themselves. So between them they reveal a wide array of internal and external factors of human action that have moral consequence. While these two outlooks conflict in theory, they complement one another in practice. In the challenge of identifying and resolving ethical dilemmas, then, neither should be ignored; each acts as a check on the limitations of the other.

Basic Values and Cardinal Goals

Victor Kraft distinguishes two components of a value concept: the character of the value—that is, its quality ("good," "bad")—and the salient feature (such as honesty or dishonesty) to which the character is attributed.[4] The quality remains the same in every scale of values—good is good and bad is bad. The differences between values inhere in their substance, and this consists in their peculiar and varying nature, both

---

4.   Victor Kraft, *Die Grundlagen einer wissenschaftlichen Wertlehre*, 2nd rev. ed. (Vienna: Springer, 1951), 107.

general (such as honesty, dishonesty) and particular (an honest piece of information). It is the general nature of the substantiating attribute that determines our attitude to it. In general we consider honesty to be a good thing and dishonesty a bad thing, deducing from that a normative commandment such as "Thou shalt not lie." But insistence on the universal validity of certain norms can conflict with the values on which they rest. To illustrate, had the (few!) people who hid Jews from the Nazis told the truth—not out of fear but out of love of truth—they would with their honesty have committed the direst of offenses against the very value of humanity that they exemplified.

Private and public valuations therefore always have to entail taking a position with reference to specific values in a specific situation; otherwise morality ends up as moralism, which trivializes everything genuinely moral. Moralism reduces ethics to banalities, makes the moral life a matter of petty discipline. It radically truncates ethical complexity into bitesize snippets of manners, handy for packaging in a canon, adherence to which calms the conscience. This is reminiscent of Albert Schweitzer's remark that a clear conscience is the invention of the devil. Moralism never shows much concern for the big questions like reason and justice. It makes no really important demands on peple's "good will."

This should not be misread as an absolutizing of what is relative. Changing situations do not suffice for determining the "good." We do, after all, need to orient ourselves on an unconditional standard, even if the norms issuing from it can only be actualized in a concrete historical situation. The critical point thus turns on the relativization of the absolute in a certain context, imparting to every moral decision the cachet of being unique and special. Everything relative requires an absolute norm as an ultimate point of reference. That is why special cases cannot be used to justify negating universally valid values and norms. Otherwise everyone could claim to be an exception, which would amount to a contradiction in terms.

The problem this raises is well illustrated by the hotly contested topic of euthanasia. With an eye to cases where excruciating agony can only end in a painful death, many protagonists of euthanasia deem it necessary to enact legislation that in the last analysis would be tantamount to absolutizing the relative value of life. When it is argued, for example, that *someone else's* life is no longer worth living for that person, or when conventional pronouncements on the meaning of life are parroted, all too often assumptions are pressed into service that the ascertainable facts fail to warrant. Actually, it is wrong to speak of a value judgment at all, since what is being expressed is a position springing from the feeling of the moment, an emotion (however motivated), a "moral" state of mind, and as such completely devoid of value consciousness. Positions are grounded in concrete, temporally contingent individual experiences and are therefore extremely diverse and ambivalent. Values, in contrast, are consistent and timeless—the goals to which morality aspires, lending it a purpose. In the goals resides the unconditional normative premise from which morality derives its justification or its disqualification—or simply, its purpose.

In saying this we are not advocating an ethics that admits any goals and means whatever and does not distinguish between good and evil. There are means that "desanctify" the end and are therefore not expedient, and there are ends that are not worthy of sanctified means. In order to preclude arbitrariness, the cardinal goals that human beings universally aspire to need to be identified. Among them are *life, freedom of action*, and *solidarity*. Failing their fulfillment, all other goals would be unattainable, or at least the possibility of attaining them would shrivel to an extent matching the shortfall in satisfying the cardinal preconditions fully.

Now there may be those who object that *life*—their own—means nothing to them. Every person has to decide for himself or herself on what to make of his or her life. "But if he bids the will to live to turn into the will not to live ... he comes into conflict with himself," wrote Schweitzer. "He elevates something unnatural, something intrinsically untrue and impossible of realization, to his world view and philosophy of life." And this is shot through with inconsistencies, because notwithstanding its negation of the world and of life, it can do nothing other than make concessions to life; otherwise it would have to lead to suicide. Affirmation of life, in contrast, aims "to create values and bring about advances that serve to augment the material, spiritual and ethical development of the human being and humankind."[5]

As for *freedom of action*, many people are either not free to exercise it fully—children, for example—or else do not want it. This does not mean, however, that they relinquish their freedom to decide, but rather that they submit to those whom they feel to be superior. Also, limits must be placed on efforts aimed at realizing this goal in order not to constrict others' freedom of action.

---

5.   Albert Schweitzer, *Aus meinem Leben und Denken* (Stuttgarter Hausbücherei, no year), 153ff.

From which it clearly follows that solidarity must also be counted as a cardinal human goal. Children depend on the *solidarity* of adults for their development into mature free agents. People who feel they are too weak to fight for their interests need the solidarity of others to stand up for their rights without being oppressed in turn. But everyone else depends on solidarity too. It is easily overlooked that a Robinson Crusoe or a hermit is able to eke out his existence only thanks to the traditional knowledge he received from his forebears. So solitary existence also hinges on cooperation.

Binding, as the primary goals may be, we must not forget how difficult, and sometimes impossible, it is to live up to the holistic responsibility they entail, which involves not only other human beings but the world around them as well. As Albert Schweitzer wrote:

> "The world presents the gruesome spectacle of the will to live sundering itself. One existence prevails at the expense of another; one destroys the other. Only in the thinking human being has the will to live come to awareness of others so willed and to the will to join them in solidarity. But in practice he cannot do so completely because man, too, is in thrall to the enigmatic and terrible law that compels him to live at the expense of other life and to make himself culpable by destroying and harming life. As an ethical being, however, he struggles to escape this compulsion wherever he can."[6]

With his life-ethos, then, Schweitzer is not propounding an impracticable, absolute kind of asceticism, for humans are no more able than animals to survive without harming or destroying plant life at the least. The decisive point for him is that an awareness of primary values should be kindled again and again, since failing this, any ethics becomes worn and watered down in the course of time, leading eventually to despondent fatalism. But affirmation of life, of freedom and solidarity, embraces optimistic willing and hoping. It does not shrink from "seeing dismal reality as what it is." In Schweitzer's ethics of life there is "no destiny for humankind other than the one humankind itself forges by dint of its convictions."[7]

With his ethics of Reverence for Life, Albert Schweitzer gives the most concrete answer to the question of what constitutes the fundamental principle of morality. His ethics comes most directly to grips

---

6.   Ibid. 155.
7.   Albert Schweitzer, *Kultur und Ethik,* spec. ed. (Munich: C.H. Beck, 1981), 330.

with reality and with individual experience, based as it is on this oftquoted perception:

> "I am life that wants to live, in the midst of life that wants to live…Just as in my will to live there is the longing to go on living and for the mysterious elation of the will to live called pleasure, and the dread extermination and the mysterious vitiation of the will to live called pain: thus it is in the will to live that surrounds me also, whether it can express this to me or remains mute."[8]

Taken to heart, this insight gives rise naturally to principles of behavior that are absolutely binding and as such the foundation on which the most diverse ethical obligations rest: "good" is everything that preserves life, fosters it, brings it to its peak worth; "evil" is everything that tears down life, does it harm, or hampers its development.

In consonance with Schweitzer's outlook, the philosopher and management consultant Rupert Lay proposes the concept of "biophilia" in the context of his discussion of business ethics. A successful life, he suggests, can be measured in terms of the "biophilic harvest" that a person reaps over a lifetime.[9] This harvest he defines thus:

> "My actions and decisions are biophilic to the extent that in and through them I enhance rather than diminish personal life in all its dimensions—emotional, social, vocational performance, moral, religious, intellectual, artistic—in my own life and others' lives, or else lay the groundwork making such enhancement possible."[10]

This principle we adopt in our exposition of business ethics by affirming as desirable everything that a business can undertake to augment rather than abridge personal life in all its dimensions. This demands a business ethos "that does not ignore economic efficiency yet also sets its sights on humanity, that affirms achievement and self-realization while also encompassing responsibility and self-commitment," as Hans Küng once put it.[11]

---

8.   Ibid.
9.   R. Lay, *Ich halte die Zeit an. Ein Buch, zu sich selbst zu finden* (Hildesheim: Bernward Publishers, 1991), 10.
10. Ibid.
11. Hans Küng, "Lebensstandard ist kein Ersatz für Lebenssinn," in Alfred Herrhausen Society for International Dialogue Ltd. (ed.), *Arbeit der Zukunft—Zukunft der Arbeit*, (Frankfurt a.M., 1994).

Business Morality and Business Ethics

In discussing the norms that govern the conduct of businesses, we use—in analogy with the distinction already drawn between morality and ethics—the concept "corporate morality." This term epitomizes the values and standards that are recognized as binding within a company. Corporate ethics analyzes the values and norms that actually hold sway in a company and inquires into the qualitative aspects that make its way of doing things "good." As applied ethics, it seeks to establish, through cooperation with the people affected by what a company does, material and procedural norms that the company then carries prescriptively into effect. The object is to circumscribe the conflict laden repercussions of the profit principle through a mechanism of control over concrete company operations. The broad basic idea underlying this approach is that of a social contract, in accordance with which all members of a society act in harmony and show consideration for the iterests of others.

The cardinal goals that are valid for the individual apply to a company as well: its existence, freedom to operate, and solidarity, understood in the sense of cooperation and of acting as a responsible corporate citizen in the global society. Accordingly, corporate ethics can only refer to the kinds of actions and measures that are compatible with the assured existence of the company in the market or that do not imperil it. A company has to have the freedom to operate, for without that every economic initiative—and in consequence economic progress—would be crippled. And a company requires the cooperation of every participant in the business process, since without them it could not accomplish the other primary goals. Just as in the individual sphere, however, a company's cardinal goals come up against limits wherever the secured existence and the freedom of others are jeopardized. A company also has the obligation to cooperate or to manifest its solidarity with people—that is, it must act with a care for the public welfare as well as its self-interest.

The question of whether businesses, in striving to be profitable, are subject to prevailing moral laws has long since been answered in the affirmative. The business world, too, affirms that it bears responsibility for more than just company financial results. Many companies emphasize the interface between business activity and society at large and the need to strike a balance between economic, social, and ecological responsibilities. The consensus today is that it is incumbent on all segments of society, companies included, to contribute to sustainable development. At the very least, they should refrain from any form of conduct that runs counter to this aim. Sustainable development requires that economic, social, and ecological concerns (the so called "triple bottom line") should not be treated as isolated matters, and certainly not played off against each other.

There is no special morality for business organizations, or for multinational companies. Expectations about how multinationals should conduct themselves tend to be more broadly defined, however. In comparison with national and local companies, internationally active businesses undoubtedly possess a number of advantages—capital strength, technology, skills, a broad geographic base, and in many cases research—that could be said to give them greater "power." At the same time, however, the indisputable correlate of greater power is a heightened acceptance of responsibility. Thus in view of their economic clout and the advantages just described, which they normally enjoy along with their transnational experience, multinational corporations do have to accept a greater responsibility. That is why, for example, competitiveness with local firms in sectors like personnel costs, outlays for safety, marketing, and other ticklish areas is but one relevant dimension bearing on decisions. A further dimension must be taken into account in every decision—namely, superordinate criteria that legitimize it ethically.

To set right the myth of "profits," and most especially profitable business doings in developing countries, it must be emphasized again and again that in order to translate moral standards into practice, every company ultimately depends on being able to show a profit after covering its costs. The relationship between moral behavior and profitable business dealings is not an either-or matter. Neither profit as such nor its magnitude are the critical point in an ethical analysis, but rather how it was arrived at and whether the profit principle was properly applied in the circumstances. The relevant quality criteria include such indices as good sense, competence, and fairness. Protestant theologian Arthur Rich's prefatory remarks to his discussion of economic ethics apply equally to corporate ethics: "Every endeavor to exert ethical influence on how the economy is structured and on the conduct of those active in it must pay regard to what is economically apposite. Anything diametrically opposed to this can never be ethically defensible."[12]

Economic and managerial competence is therefore always a necessary condition and the "pre-requisite of the ought."[13] Ethical

12. A. Rich, *Marktwirtschaft, Planwirtschaft, Weltwirtschaft aus sozialethischer Sicht,* Wirtschaftsethik II (Gütersloh: Gerd Mohn, 1990), 16.

13. H. Lenk and M. Maring (eds.), *Wirtschaft und Ethik* (Stuttgart: Reclam, 1992), 12.

competence does not supplant economic competence, or vice versa. Company earnings are necessary not only for reasons of business management; they also have socio-ethical significance. The operative success of a business serves to secure productive jobs, the provision of important goods and services, and the development of new technologies. Profits further allow economic, social, and ecological investments and, through the tax revenues realized from them, make an important contribution to financing public expenditures. Where a constructive political and social climate exists, these corporate contributions are of instrumental value in augmenting the public welfare. Indeed, in a world of continuing high absolute population growth and shrinking resources[14], economic success can be termed ethically imperative. Losses do not just lack any "ethical" value—they hurt the business that posts them and are a hindrance to social progress.

Corporate ethics and the moral claims derived from them do not call into question the basic economic function that corporations perform. They are the ancillary element by which the quality criterion "morality" is strived for in carrying out that function. Ethical criteria permeate the process of defining management objectives and of setting priorities, while ethical queries and probes provide a kind of quality control with respect to the ways in which business objectives should be achieved. Just as enlightened environmental management today is no longer "end of the pipe"—that is, a cleanup operation as the last step in the production process—applied corporate ethics has to be understood as an integral part of the whole scene of operations, in the sense of systems management. The voluntarily assumed commitments attest to a realization that neither the "invisible hand" of the market nor the prevailing legal system suffice to preclude conflictladen outgrowths of the profit principle. In all cases the aim remains to make corporate activity more effective and efficient.

2. Ethics Beyond Borders

Hardly any growing business can today afford to think in non-global terms. The most challenging area of thinking in this field is that of global ethics. Global business requires an ethical approach more complex than either wholly embracing the ethical norms of whatever society in which the company functions or simply adhering to one code of conduct

---

14. Klaus M. Leisinger, Karin Schmitt, Rajul Pandya-Lorch, *Six Billion and Counting. Population and Food Security in the 21st Century*, International Food Policy Research Institute (ed.), (Washington, D.C.: Johns Hopkins University Press, 2002).

throughout the company, irrespective of differing society or culture. In the global economy, if we are going to write rules of behavior, those rules must be framed in the context of world citizenry so that employees have the ability to adapt to local customs yet comply with the values that define the corporate character.

Certainly, notions of acceptable business conduct differ widely across national boundaries. What Northern Europe and North America castigate as bribery and corruption, is the normal way of prioritizing and facilitating transactions in substantial sections of the Third World; and what the West considers to be the normal fee for the rental of money, is condemned by fundamentalist Islam as usury. In the face of these and all other actual cultural variations, and the common but fundamentally mistaken view that tolerance presupposes *ethical relativism*, proponents of business ethics have typically been unwilling to make universal pronouncements. To some extent this reflects an appropriate diffidence: if all they have to assert is a personal, institutional or a national preference, or a codification of local practice, then attempts to impose those attitudes universally would indeed be presumptuous.

That there are varieties of moralities and moral codes is a fact that is not in question. Ethical relativism, however, is not a fact, but a theory that attempts to account for this fact. The fact of moral diversity is of course a main source of this theory, since it provides the data that it tries to explain. But by itself it is not sufficient to give rise to it or to establish it. For this purpose other assumptions are required, and these cannot themselves be established.

This theory arises, in the first place, from a failure to distinguish moral rules, and particular moral judgments, from moral principles. It involves a failure to distinguish the invariant moral principles from the variable conditions that, in accordance with these principles, require or permit a variety of different rules and practices. Moral principles do not require any uniformity of practices in different cultures or in different circumstances. What is right in one context or set of circumstances may not be right in another, and differences in social or geographical conditions, or in social or cultural needs, can count as relevant differences in circumstances. However, though practices and rules may be "relative," it does not follow that principles are.

In the second place, this theory also arises out of the assumption that if a certain practice prevails in a certain place then it is necessarily right in that place, that if a rule is not *recognized* or *observed* by the members of a certain group then it does not *apply* to or is not *binding* on the members of that group. This assumption is not only peculiar; it leads to contradiction. There is no reason why this assumption must be restricted to a group or a society, if it holds for a group then it would hold for any individual. On this assumption, one could organize a group of thieves, who, by the mere fact that they like or want to steal, would be justified in stealing. Indeed, on this view one could justify oneself in doing anything whatsoever merely by refusing to recognize any rule against it or by inculcating a taste for it. No one is justified in violating any moral rule, or in violating the rights of another, simply because he wants to or finds it convenient, or simply because he has no scruples against it; and no one would be justified in this simply because he is a member of a group with similar dispositions.

Since moral principles, by definition, transcend the geographical and temporal boundaries of particular societies, and hence all merely local needs and conditions, there is nothing to which they could be "relative," except to morality itself. The fact that in some places, or by some people, a certain principle may not be recognized or accepted is purely irrelevant. So is the fact that there might be someone who does not accept or act in accordance with *any* moral principles. Such a person would be immoral, but this has no more bearing on the validity of moral principles than the existence of fallacious reasoning has on the validity of logical principles.

From this follows that, as a by-product of the global economy, the global corporation must envision a set of core values and a mission that are in line with general moral principles. A good candidate for the global corporation's core values are those found in the Aristotelian code of ethics—wisdom, courage, selfcontrol, and justice. Aristotle's philosophical system also provides a mission for the global corporation: the pursuit of global harmony, the spread of economic democracy, the distribution of the benefits of globalization not just among its constituent units but among the members of the world community, and the material and spiritual prosperity of humankind.

A global ethic for the global economy provides a framework for morally responsible business habits, but the day-to-day practice requires customization and nurturing highly specific, highly personal competencies. Although all companies may subscribe to a global ethic, the terms of participation will vary according to the conditions confronting that particular organization and its own maturity, confidence and culture. Consider the United Nations Charter of Rights. Written in

1948, this document encoded the principles of human dignity that were largely derived from the institutions, constitutions and charters of the democracies that had defeated fascism in the Second World War. The majority of the world's nations, involving countless other social and political traditions, did not necessarily have the same mores regarding the value and potential of an individual person. At various speeds and to varying degrees of commitment, the appreciation of, and aspiration to, these human rights has grown around the world. Most countries now include the principles of human rights in their own charters and constitutions. These are highly varied in their structure, expression and practice, but the point is that there is an orientation, an inexorable progress, toward fulfilling the intent of the UN Charter. That it is an irregular progress, that some of it is more cosmetic than substantial, and that it is not a universal, does not diminish the truth or benefits of that continuous achievement since 1948.

Similarly, companies that adopt a global ethic are subscribing to an aspiration that will tolerate and require endless variety in practice. Hans Küng makes two critical points in this regard. First, he reminds us of the reality that "as in the question of human rights or ecology, or peace and disarmament, and the partnership of men and women, this [global ethic] will happen in a very complex and long-drawn-out process of change in consciousness."[15]

There is an urgency to assume responsibility, an urgency that grows with environmental degradation and social displacement, but it is a responsibility that each individual, group and company must fashion, define and assume for itself. If this seems unreasonable, we need only review the spread of environmental consciousness, which within a generation has gone from the radical fringe to the global mainstream. This evolution is neither easy nor automatic, but it represents a new, learned habituation that is still growing in momentum and influence.

Küng's second point is that "a global ethic does not mean a new global ideology, or even an attempt to arrive at one uniform religion. The call for a global ethic does not aim to replace the supreme ethical demands of each individual religion with an ethical minimalism; it is not meant to take the place of the Torah, the Sermon on the Mount, the Qur'an, the Bhagavad-Gita, the Discourses of the Buddha or the Sayings of Confucius."[16] In corporate terms, this means that a global ethic is not a

---

15. Hans Küng (ed.), *Yes to a Global Ethic* (New York: Continuum, 1996), 3.
16. Ibid.

replacement for strategy or culture but a consciousness that is integrated into the company to affect both. The goal is not a single, standardized conformity, but a deepening of the awareness, and a widening of the corporate habit, for ethical consideration and accountability.

3. Corporate Social Responsibility

Over the past 25 years, the view that business enterprises as "legal persons" have moral rights and duties that previously were associated only with "natural persons" has become increasingly accepted. In the framework of the law and of the competitive scene, corporations lay claim to economic, social, and ecological rights whose natural correlates are corresponding obligations. These include, notably:

- a commitment to the short- and long-term welfare of the company;
- responsible and scrupulous treatment of employees;
- customer satisfaction;
- manufacture of reasonably priced, useful, safe, healthful (or nontoxic) quality products, with services to match;
- the creation or at least preservation of workplaces;
- corporate social performance; and
- due regard to shareholder value—to the short-and long-term interests of those who invest their money in the company.

Companies are rated against this checklist of public expectations, though the priority assigned to the component obligations fluctuates in reaction to the economic, social, and ecological conditions of the day. Thus during the past 30 years, probably not least because of the favorable economic situation, environmental and social issues have gained steadily in importance in the eyes of society. Since the mid-1960s, interest in the social and ecological quality of business activity in developing countries has likewise been rising. Special interest groups—the so-called NGOs (nongovernmental organizations)—that focus mainly on developing-world problems have grown in importance, and they demand a degree of social and ecological responsibility from companies oriented to the global market.

"Social" responsibility is understood here as "societal" responsibility—that is, a responsibility toward society in general. While the standard defining a social responsibility also depends on the local context, any definition encompasses responsibilities with differing degrees of obligation. A distinction can be drawn among what is:

- required of business by society—the "must do" dimension of social responsibility, which by societal consensus goes without saying and is the minimum standard necessary for a corporation's sustainable existence;
- expected of business by society—the "ought to do" dimension of social responsibility, which is less binding but which most people in modern societies still regard as largely a matter of course; and
- desired of business by society—the "can do" dimension of social responsibility, the fulfillment of which deserves public praise, although a company not delivering in this area would not have to fear public blame.

We are presenting here our personal view of the matter and explicitly want to go beyond the moral minimum. To be as specific as possible, we discuss Corporate Social Responsibility in the context of a pharmaceutical enterprise.

A sustainable solution to today's poverty and health problems in Subsaharan Africa and other poverty-ridden regions can only be expected if all actors show goodwill and accept a level of responsibility that extends beyond their positions to date. What is also needed is leadership in relation to creative and innovative ways of opening up new avenues with corporate social responsibility.

The "Must Do" Dimension

The dimension of responsibility that by social consensus is nonnegotiable for the pharmaceutical industry and many others is no different today than in the past: to provide goods and services that effectively meet customer demands and that can be sold at prices that are competitive and in the best interest of the corporation. This has to be achieved in compliance with law as well as in harmony with human rights and workers' rights, and with minimal impacts of unintended externalities.

The goods and services that are sold provide society with different kinds of value added—in the case of pharmaceuticals, they prevent premature death and disability, accelerate cure, or alleviate the symptoms of diseases for which there is so far no cure. Being a successful pharmaceutical corporation therefore means not only being profitable, but also raising the quality of life of sick people, avoiding costly hospitalization, and allowing people to go back to normal working lives instead of being bedridden.

If and when it can deliver on these basic societal expectations and do it with sustained profitability resulting from sustained competitiveness on global markets, a corporation is able to be a good corporate citizen—that is, on a sustainable basis, to

- promote invention and ingenuity to cope with the challenges of a growing world population;
- hire, keep, develop, and competitively remunerate employees;
- pay taxes;
- contribute toward pension and insurance systems; and
- support other social purposes.

Drawing attention to this "must do" dimension of societal responsibility is not the boring chore of someone whose salary is paid by the pharmaceutical industry. While not subscribing fully to Milton Friedman's famous view that the business of business is business only, and that a corporation has no further obligations as long as it obeyed the law, we share Friedman's concern that bringing human and social values into economic decisions will lead ultimately to a shift from market mechanism to political mechanisms.[17] At times when the judgment of a just societal division of labor seems to be so blurred, such a wake-up call to reality is a political necessity; it creates transparency about what can be expected on a sustainable basis. At times when expectations are growing wildly, it is also fair to once in a while go on record pointing out that private business has a right to be profitoriented, to protect its investments, and to be compensated for innovation.

Having said this, we are, of course, aware that modern societies expect more and better, such as in the context of essential and life-saving drugs for individually poor patients in collectively poor countries. It is obvious that legitimate efforts to achieve profit and the insistence on intellectual property rights can, under certain circumstances, come into conflict with the "right to life" of someone living in dire poverty. And it is equally clear that it cannot be the duty of a company to give away valuable goods if those who need them cannot afford to buy them. Complex problems do not have simple solutions, and promising approaches presuppose that those who can contribute a stone to the mosaic of the overall solution do so in cooperation with others.

---

17. M. Friedman, "The Social Responsibility of Business is to Increase its Profits," in *New York Times Magazine* (13 September 1970); see also M. Friedman, "The Social Responsibility of Business," in Beauchamp T.L., Bowie N.E. (eds.), *Ethical Theory and Busienss* (New Jersey: Prentice-Hall, 1983), 81–83.

The "Ought To Do" Dimension

Most people in modern societies expect that responsible companies avoid questionable pratices and respond to the "spirit" of law rather than a narrow interpretation of the letter of law, such as by paying "living wages" and protecting the environment in countries where this is not legally required—corporate behavior as, for example, demanded by the UN Global Compact. (See Chapter 11.)

For the research-based pharmaceutical industry, other dimensions become relevant in addition. Two are of special importance: flexibility for negotiated, differential pricing according to specific needs and demands, and the readiness to help out with donations in cases of acute emergency.

While donations in the case of emergencies are relatively easy to determine, and misuse is less frequent, differential pricing for different markets needs some additional measures to prevent an exploitation of goodwill. Control over trade is required to avoid re-exportation or leakage of the low-priced drugs to the markets of industrial countries. It also requires an appropriate political environment, including a readiness on the part of consumers in high-priced markets to accept sustained price differences. Moreover, it may also require undertakings from industrial countries not to use differential prices intended only for poor countries as benchmarks for their own price regulation systems or policies.

The "Can Do" Dimension of Social Responsibility

The "desirable" actions constitute a dimension of social responsibility that is neither required by law nor standard industry practice. Delivery on the "can do" norms of social responsibility will not protect a company whose actual operations do not comply with the law or other aspects of the "must do" dimension. And yet, it can nevertheless offer people substantial social or other advantages.

Desired actions are, for example, social benefits through subsidiaries situated in poor countries, such as free or heavily subsidized meals for workers and employees, nursery schools for single mothers, free training opportunities using company infrastructure, or scholarship programs for the children of employees in low-income groups. The extras may also take the form of providing free or heavily subsidized facilities for diagnosis, treatment, and psychosocial care for employees with HIV/AIDS or other poverty-related diseases such as TB or malaria.

Corporate philanthropy, defined as expenditure beyond a company's actual business activities without any specific association with direct corporate advantages and without any financially measurable rewards in return, is regarded by some stakeholders with skepticism, because these are benefits that are voluntary and can also be cut back again—for example, when the climate in the business environment gets harsher.

Given widespread poverty and the major human suffering associated with it, even if a company does nothing more than act purely as a financial sponsor for humanitarian purposes, this should be acknowledged as laudable. Normally, however, in addition to their financial resources, companies also have a wealth of knowledge and experience at their disposal that they can put to great use by investing in projects and programs of development cooperation and humanitarian aid to increase effectiveness, efficiency, and significance. As part of such projects, a company may donate medicines—just as Novartis, for example, has done by signing a memorandum of understanding with WHO to provide free treatment for all leprosy patients in the world until the disease has been eliminated from every country—but also may invest in social development programs to enhance the absorptive and institutional capacity of the recipients. The establishment and endowment of corporate foundations with a humanitarian purpose can also be seen in the context of "can do" norms.

Companies that become engaged in this way create the opportunity to become competent regarding problems of poverty and familiar with poverty-elated realities—experiences that do not otherwise form part of the normal cosmos of a company. As a result, a company's understanding grows with regard to completely different viewpoints, and the company gains in terms of social competence—this is structurally different from any kind of "do gooderism" triggered by public pressure in a given critical situation.

Contributions from the research efforts of the pharmaceutical industry also fall into the category of "can do" norms of social responsibility. This may, for example, follow the approach of the Novartis Institute for Tropical Diseases in Singapore, where—in collaboration with others as a joint public-private initiative—*pro bono* research is conducted into the dis-eases of poverty such as tuberculosis and dengue fever.

Or it could take the form of creating a Consultative Group on International Health Research. Research-based pharmaceutical companies could pass on to this institution any chemical compounds that offered justified hope for pharmacological effects on diseases of poverty but that the companies do not intend to develop further because the expected indication does not lie in an area the company wishes to focus market efforts on. Various actors in civil society could provide the resources for further R&D, whether in the form of national or multilateral development aid or through NGOs.

4. Corruption's Corrosive Influence

Corruption is a problem that in varying degrees besets societies all over the world. Hans-Ludwig Zachert, head of the German Federal Bureau of Criminal Investigation, has likened the corruption in his country to corrosion: at first it only crops up here and there, frequently making inroads beneath the surface. "No matter how much government apologists may maintain otherwise," he has stated, "corruption in the public service is not just a matter of 'a few black sheep' but an alarmingly everyday occurrence in Germany."[18]

According to Zachert, the main profiteer is organized crime, which, aided by civil servants on the take, seeks to gain massive influence over the authorities. "Practically no sector is spared corruption or quasi-corrupt practices. Hardly a day passes without new cases coming to light."[19] If timely countermeasures are not set in motion, he fears, the canker will become so widespread as to subvert the very pillars of the system.

In emergent economies such as South Korea or Mexico, former top officeholders are suspected of or have been arrested for corruption; likewise in France, Italy, Belgium, and Japan. American analyses see corruption as a widespread problem in the United States too. Publications from the United Kingdom, Japan, and the Netherlands, as well as a voluminous documentation on Italian "tagentopoli" (more than 1,300 top managers were taken into custody), fuel the supposition that virtually every society on earth knows corruption in one guise or another.[20] The Council of the Organization for Economic Co-operation and Development (OECD) has recommended that every member of the

---

18. Cited in P. Scherer, "Korruption fast alltäglich," in *Die Welt*, no. 40-7, (16 February 1995): 1.

19. Ibid.

20. See the *TI-Newsletters*, Transparency International e.V. (ed.), Heylstrasse 33, 10825 Berlin, Germany.

'club' of affluent industrial countries take effective measures to deter, prevent, and combat corruption in international business operations.[21]

The global dimension of the corruption phenomenon stands proved, as does the fact that no country in the world claims it is a desirable way of doing things compatible with the general welfare. But how is the phenomenon to be clearly defined?

First off, without beating about the bush or prettifying the subject, corruption can be defined as the misuse of power for private benefit. The power may, but need not, reside in the public domain. Besides money, the benefit can take the form of protection, special treatment, commendation, promotion, or the favors of women or men.

A more refined approach discloses a remarkably complex cluster of mores that is judged quite differently from culture to culture and, in terms of its ramifications, accordingly heterogeneous. In some cultures, gifts and reciprocal favors are part of the code of expected conduct and social behavior. In others, the person who wishes to show gratitude for professional assistance rendered by offering a personal gift can quickly bring discredit on himself or herself as well as on the beneficiary.

Whereas some countries permit bribes to be deducted from taxes as "operating expenses" or "special outlays," others—such as the United States—have anticorruption legislation that even makes the bribing of foreign nationals in a foreign country a punishable offense. For companies based in different parts of the world, this legislative confusion leaves varying degrees of latitude for coming to terms with corruption. For this reason, it is useful to go over the problem in the context of corporate ethics. In a nutshell, corruption has four main distinguishing features:

- misuse of a position of power;
- gaining of advantage for those who, actively and passively, are parties of the misuse;
- undesirable effects on third parties (ramifications); and
- secrecy.

Since both the dimensions of a position of power and the advantages and undesirable consequences can vary greatly, we need to differentiate further. Before turning to consider the moral differences among the

---

21. *Recommendation of the Council of the OECD on Bribery in International Business Transactions* (Paris, September 1994).

various forms of corruption, a couple of further observations. First, not all businesses are susceptible to it in like degree. Construction firms that specialize in infrastructure and other large-scale projects and manufacturers of big-ticket capital equipment such as turbines or aircraft are especially vulnerable, particularly when the decision on a contract hinges on just a few people or even on one person alone. Ailing companies with uncompetitive products and services are more inclined to stoop to corrupt behavior than are healthy companies that enjoy a salient marketing edge thanks to excellent products and services.

The often heard blanket statements about "the" developing countries and about "everyone" in them in a position of responsibility or authority being prone to corruption are wrong. True, in some countries corruption tainted payments may be more widespread and more often involve officeholders, and to that extent be a condition of doing business successfully. This does not mean, however, that corruption is practiced universally in developing countries or that honest officials are nowhere to be found.

The Forms Corruption Can Take

To begin with, it is important to draw a purely quantitative distinction between "small" and "big" corruption. In addition, we need to distinguish whether the intended end, whatever dimension corruption may take, is licit or illicit.

"Petty" Corruption: "Every Victory over Hopelessness has Its Price."
This form is characterized by small payments made to induce someone empowered to take a decision to get on with it more quickly. The payments are made because without this extra "stimulus" nothing would happen; or else the desired action would be unconscionably delayed, which is why they are known as "speed-up gratuities." The word "petty" refers to both the size of the financial incentive and the extent of the obligation that the transaction buys.

In many poor countries, petty corruption pervades every segment of society. Where poverty is rampant, many people may be forced in their daily struggle to survive to do things that they would not need to do if they were better off. In this light, petty corruption appears as a kind of social survival strategy. The person who takes a firm line in resisting demands for a bribe will find work impeded. Sometimes this can be offset by extra personal effort, sometimes not. "Each person has to find out for himself how clean he wants to stay—and how firm he can remain," noted an employee of the Swiss Directorate for Development and Cooperation (SDC).[22] A case history from Mexico illustrates the consequences that can ensue from a show of firmness:

In the early 1990's, it was hard all over the country to obtain a telephone extension. The price set by Teléfonos de Mexico, which has the monopoly, is 500 dollars, inclusive of installation. Only 5 out of 100 applicants tried this route. The rest preferred to shell out 1000 to 1500 dollars on a huge black market controlled by employees of the monopoly itself. For 1500 dollars you got your phone within days. But if you paid Teléfonos de Mexico 500 you could wait 12 months—at the least. The workers who installed the illegal extensions at incredible speed earned 400 dollars a month.[23]

A Mexican political analyst notes that "Everything can be fixed like that—whether you want to enroll a child in secondary school, evade a traffic fine or leave the country without having to show your military identity card. Every victory over hopelessness has its price."[24]

It is possible to quite rightly wax indignant about corruption tainting humanitarian aid. Yet taking every aspect into consideration, the fact is that clearcut solutions are not possible here either. A former deputy director of the SDC has admitted carrying on the mission even under conditions tarnished by corruption. "Humanitarian assistance is necessary all the same," he said. "If one were to declare that we shall cease aiding countries where corruption exists, then there would be practically nothing more we could do. But the whole point is to bring about improvements."[25]

Terminating an aid program because of "small" exactions seldom has an impact on those who are the intended beneficiaries anyway. Instead, the brunt falls on those whose chances for a better life depend, sometimes critically, on humanitarian aid and development cooperation. Here again the social consequences of alternative courses of action in a given case have to be weighed.

---

22. Statement of an SDC member working in Madagascar, see Swiss Directorate for Development and Cooperation (ed.), *Entwicklung/Developpement*, no. 38 (November 1992).
23. See C.G. Leyva, "Die Korruption blüht nach wie vor," in Swiss Directorate for Development and Cooperation (ed.), *Entwicklung/Developpement* no. 38 (November 1992): 8f.
24. Ibid. 9.
25. Ibid. 31.

Gifts

In the sphere of minor corruption, gifts present a delicate special problem. They need not always be given with ulterior motives in mind; often they are part of a culture's mores, serving as tokens of personal courtesy. In many cultures, gifts such as an invitation to dinner are frankly expected as marks of respect or as a proof of amicable relations. Refusing them can be taken as a sign of rejection or even as an affront.

In the Federal Republic and many other industrial nations, it is considered akin to corruption for a company to give its customers gifts, or at least ethically suspect. The problem lies not in giving as such, however, but in the value of what is given. Countenanced up to a certain limit, as soon as this is exceeded, the practice is looked upon askance.

Various organizations have drawn up guidelines on how their employees should act with respect to the presents they give to customers or business friends as well as any they may receive. The practice may be expressly forbidden; advice about what is appropriate may be given, or an upper limit may be specified—the value must not exceed $100, for example. Guidelines can never provide a complete solution, though, on account of such factors as a different standard of living between giver and receiver, cultural dissimilarities and divergent social norms, or quite simply the gray areas inherent in giving and receiving. What always remains is latitude of interpretation and discretion demanding an independent exercise of judgment on the part of the person involved.

The intention of the giver is always an important consideration in that exercise. If a gift is meant simply as a kindness and a friendly gesture, free of any expectation that a reciprocal situation might arise, there is little call to make an issue of it. Still, such gifts are not altogether unproblematic either, since they do serve to generate good will that can pay off later in some other connection. Sociologist S. Neckel refers in this connection to the "Don Corleone Principle," describing how subtly habit-forming gifts can get to be.[26]

In case of doubt, it is always best to neither give nor accept gifts. But a good way to stay clear of any suspicion of corruption is, for example, to

---

26. "I do you a favor and do not expect a favor in return—except, should I once need your help, I can count on you." See S. Neckel, "Der unmoralische Tausch: Eine Soziologie der Käuflichkeit," in *Kursbuch* no. 120 (Berlin: Rowohlt, 1995), 15.

have any gifts received personally made available to all the employees through a company raffle.[27] Companies and other organizations do well to take preventive action by obliging employees whose position makes them particularly exposed to temptation to inform their superiors or the company auditors of any gifts received. With the matter out in the open, a fair way of handling it can be chosen.

Large-Scale Corruption

Although the boundaries between small-scale and large-scale corruption are fluid, it is the latter that presents a distinct problem area. In the worst case, a parasitic political and economic upper crust ruthlessly capitalizes on the clout it wields to funnel huge sums into its own pockets. In order to bag loot on that scale, corrupted and corrupters shop for goods and services bearing the highest possible price tag.

Everyone involved has an interest. The supplier sells pricey, perhaps overpriced, goods and services, while the "customer" takes his cut in the form of illicit "commissions." Development ruins in many a poor country testify to the deplorable results of such wheeling and dealing. Mostly they are relatively useless, ill adapted, lavishly expensive installations, colossal prestige projects and bloated construction schemes, or else armaments that far exceed a country's legitimate defense requirements. In most cases the transaction as such was perfectly legal.

Where does the illicit nature of such machinations lie? Those in office or otherwise empowered to make decisions are disloyal to their duty to serve the public interest, all the more so where resources are generally scarce. Instead of making the most cost-effective choice—for example, by publicly inviting tenders and straightforwardly appraising the offers that come in—they give preference to the most costly variant because this will raise the potential "commission."

Since the sums thus finagled are normally very high and do not show up on any tax declaration, naturally the direct effect on the beneficiary's income is considerable—and the harm done to the public welfare usually likewise. The devious practice has added massively to the indebtedness

---

27. [Klaus M. Leisinger]: During a stint in a developing country in Africa I was, to my utter surprise, showered with gifts from customers. At the end of my first year I had them put on display in the company conference room, numbered them, and raffled them off among the full workforce. Everyone from the night guard to the secretaries to my fellow members of management got the chance to acquire desirable items that would otherwise have been beyond their means. Without wishing to insinuate that these customers hoped to point me in a certain direction, I can report that there were no more presents once the word got around about how they were distributed.

of many developing countries but seldom contributed to bettering the lot of their peoples. The upshot is the notorious "privatization of profits and socialization of losses," with the public costs of corruption outweighing whatever private benefit it may bring many times over.[28]

The privatization/socialization caper takes on especially contemptible dimensions when large-scale corruption serves illegal ends—when payments are made for the purpose of transgressing the law. As a hypothetical example, a company headquartered in an industrial country wants to spare itself the high investment costs of building an incineration plant for special wastes and mounts a search for an alternative, cheaper way to dispose of the waste. A highly placed ministry official of a developing country approaches the company with a proposal: for $3 million he will arrange for the trouble-free importation of all the waste into his country for five years. He will also see to it that the waste is "taken care of." In his village he owns ample land well suited to the purpose.

True, the import (and since the Basel Convention of 1989, the export as well) of such toxic substances is officially prohibited. But as the Deputy Minister for Economic Development, he sees no cause for worry since the waste can be mixed with other materials such as gravel or sawdust, and the waste dump would bring jobs and would therefore benefit the people of his village. Persuaded by the economic advantages of the scheme, the company assents to it.

A few years later, the people living in the vicinity of the disposal site fall victim to severe poisoning. The deputy minister swears he knew nothing of the special wastes' toxicity and was misled by the multinational. The company is indicted in the "host" country and becomes the focus of public protests in numerous industrial countries.

As noted earlier, corruption, far from being confined to developing countries, is a worldwide pestilence. But it does have especially devastating consequences in the developing world.

On Balance

Most people, and not only those of Western culture, agree that corruption is iniquitous and abhorrent. (Unless, that is, they happen to be

---

28.   J.S. Nye Jr., "Corruption and Political Development: A Cost-Benefit Analysis," in *The American Political Science Review* vol. 61 (1967): 417 ff.

among those who profit from it.) Corruption is socially destructive: it saps the foundations of honesty in society and leads to flouting of the public interest. In the marketplace, it warps competition to the point of stultification, harming the economy. Because of corruption, individuals and the state have to bear substantial costs that would otherwise not be incurred.

Corruption thwarts rational ways of getting things decided and done, putting a strain on the whole network of economic interaction—cumbersome enough in any case—in every country, but especially in developing countries. Small businesses and poor people lack the wherewithal to prod the decision-making mill to work in their interest; they are helplessly at the mercy of capriciousness and venality. So they must try to make a go of it in the outlaw zone of the shadow economy, where they live in constant fear of criminal prosecution or are forced to cough up "protection" payments to the servants of the state. As Hernando de Soto has shown, the poor of Lima, like those in other big cities in developing countries, have built up the unofficial shadow economy because "official" channels leave them no chance of survival, what with too much government and too many conditions, approvals, and decrees serving mainly to satisfy the bureaucrats' own interests and opening up opportunities for corruption to them.[29] The deleterious impact of corruption on development is beyond doubt.

The corporate world, too, can only view corruption as an evil. For one thing it undermines every effort to achieve market success by conducting a business with the customer in mind. A company that can flourish merely by greasing palms has no incentive to strive for quality. In a climate of corruption, success on the market is not determined by the quality and competitive price of products and services, but rather by how much bribe-money changes hands—not by a company's reliability and integrity and other gauges of genuine competence, but rather by the unscrupulousness of corrupt individuals. Corruption can tie up sizable financial and organizational assets that could otherwise be used elsewhere or to improve profitability—an indefensible situation.

Last, it is too much to expect of employees that they should have to perform corrupt acts. In particular, employees of multinational corporations run a big risk, because as a rule they get much more sharply censured for paying bribes than do locals. Even though two people may be doing the same thing, it is not looked on as the same at all.

---

29. Hernando de Soto, *The Other Path: The Invisible Revolution in the Third World* (Harper Collins, 1989).

No society can long subsist as an orderly whole if corrupt mores dictate the tenor of economic, civic, and political life. Widespread corruption also impedes and endangers democratization. What it always comes down to is using shady practices to procure an unfair advantage for one side at the expense of someone else. This is why a corporation that endeavors to work not only profitably but also morally above acceptable standards must have corporate guidelines that strongly discourage its employees to become involved in any direct or indirect corruption.

5. Society's View of Corporations

In the 1950s and 1960s, business still enjoyed relatively high esteem in the eyes of society at large. Current surveys indicate, however, that despite the movement toward corporate social responsibility described in Chapter 3, today more and more people believe that companies and their top managers are morally suspect and unscrupulous in their pursuit of profit. This perception is not without some basis in reality, as described in Chapter 4. Twenty years ago, *U.S. News & World Report* published the results of an investigation showing that over the preceding decade almost one fourth of the Fortune 500 companies had been either indicted for or found guilty of grave violations of the law. The 25 biggest companies, the elite of Corporate America, were conspicuous for particularly flagrant conduct.[30] No wonder that by the early 1980s American commentators were writing about a "moral crisis in American capitalism."[31]

For some years now the Washington, D.C., weekly *Corporate Crime Reporter* has listed the real or putative transgressions of various companies. What comes to light there week after week on the U.S. scene alone is nothing short of scandalous. The register of corporate iniquity compiled by the *Corporate Crime Reporter* has run the gamut from deliberate pollution, tax evasion, and deceiving the authorities through use of child labor to culpable homicide by reason of inadequate workplace safety. The fact that large companies are looked at more skeptically than small ones has, we suspect, more to do with their greater visibility and supposed power than with tangible evidence against them.

Recently the scandals have moved from the pages of the specialist *Corporate Crime Reporter* to the front pages of prominent newspapers.

---

30. O. Kelly, "Corporate Crime: The Untold Story," in *U.S. News & World Report* (September 6, 1982): 25-29.
31. R. Wuthnow, "The moral crisis in American capitalism," in *Harvard Business Review* (March, April 1982): 76-84.

The stunning news from WorldCom that it artificially inflated its earnings by $3.8 billion US is just the latest in a rash of scandals that have rocked the corporate world and shaken investors' confidence in stock markets. Criminal accounting practices (e.g. Enron[32], Tyco[33]), insider trading scandals (e.g. ImClone/Martha Stewart[34]) and allegations of outright fraud (e.g. Bre-X[35], YBM Magnex[36]) have all hit the markets in recent years.

In the German Federal Republic, publications label executives "washouts in pin stripes" and censure them for "increasing criminalization."[37] One author accuses managers of unscrupulous pursuit of selfish interests to the detriment of the firm, a fixation on coasting along and hanging onto power, logrolling and cronyism, and corruption— to which for good measure he adds mediocre intelligence, lack of discipline, and inadequate professional competence.[38]

---

32. At one time the seventh-largest company in the U.S., Enron announced in November 2001 that it had overstated its earnings back to 1997 by about $600 million US. The company camouflaged a huge debt in a web of "off balance sheet" partnerships. The company collapsed in the biggest bankruptcy filing in U.S. corporate history. The shares now trade for pennies on the over-the-counter market.

33. The conglomerate company abandoned plans to split into four parts when concerns arose over its accounting practices in the wake of the Enron fiasco. In early June, the company announced the resignation of its CEO Dennis Kozlowski, who was later charged for allegedly avoiding payment of over $1 million US in sales taxes on $13.2 million US in artwork. Tyco shares are down 80 per cent since the start of the year.

34. The drug company's cofounder and former CEO Sam Waksal and his daughter Aliza were charged June 12 with insider trading relating to sales of ImClone stock in the days leading up to the release of a federal ruling that rejected the company's new cancer drug. Martha Stewart, the diva of home decorating, came under investigation after she sold nearly 4,000 shares of ImClone on Dec. 27, a day before the regulator's announcement. She is a friend of Waksal's and shared the same stockbroker. ImClone shares are off more than 90 per cent from their highs; Martha Stewart Living Omnimedia shares have fallen 40 per cent in less than a month.

35. Calgary-based Bre-X touted in the mid-1990s that it had discovered the world's largest gold deposit in Indonesia, which sent the company's share price flying. But by the spring of 1997, new tests from the site showed there was little or no gold at the site. The initial samples that showed rich gold deposits had been spiked. The company's geologist, Michael de Guzman, died mysteriously when he fell from a helicopter into the Indonesian jungle. President David Walsh died of a brain aneurysm at his home in the Bahamas. The stock, which had been worth more than $200 a share, became worthless. The OSC is prosecuting former company executive John Felderhof for alleged insider trading.

36. The OSC is pursuing action against YBM Magnex officials over allegations they knew or should have known that the company was nothing more than a shell for Russian organized crime. Its shares are now worthless.

37. G. Ogger, *Nieten in Nadelstreifen. Deutschlands Manager im Zwielicht* (Munich: Droemer, 1992), 67.

38. Ibid.

If we take the literature from the 1990's as evidence of how corporate morality and the morality of those entrusted with responsibility in business and politics are perceived, then in the German Federal Republic, for example, there would appear to be a growing climate of "small-bore chumminess and cliquishness, of calculating rulebreaking and disloyalty, of heedless cleverness."[39] The picture that emerges is not one we would necessarily associate with a highly developed industrial country; it is more suggestive of feudally structured states somewhere far away in the economically and socially "backward" corners of the world. We read of politicians who have "shamelessly lined their own pockets or in their unbridled greed have indulged in nepotism" and, although names are named, no one has yet taken legal steps to refute the charges.[40]

Managers, other critics declare, are anything but leaders of integrity and responsible custodians of the human, financial, and other resources placed in their care. No, they are "swindlers, cutpurses, scoundrels and psychopaths obsessed with their own gain."[41] We read—and again, names are named—of how the executive suite set misappropriates company funds to fix up private holiday villas, for luxury journeys, for fatuous ostentation to the end of appeasing personal vanity and avarice.

Even when specimens of this parasitic coterie are caught and proof of their clandestine wheeling and dealing is brought to public light, they do not automatically have to reckon with sanctions, dismissal, or incarceration. Instead, by dint of recourse to the old boy network of political officeholders and other influential guardian angels, the charges are watered down, trial proceedings are stalled, and punishment is foiled. Remember that all this is not in a developing country somewhere in Africa, Asia, or Latin America, but in the heart of Europe, in one of the economically most sophisticated nations on the earth.

Under such circumstances, public prosecutors see top executives as possessing a "particularly dangerous power potential" and cite the "criminality of those who wield economic power."[42] German sociologists take "industrial fatalism" and "organized irresponsibility" as their premise; psychologists see an increase in the number of overstretched

---

39. F. Bräuninger and M. Hasenbeck, *Die Abzocker. Selbstbedienung in Politik und Wirtschaft* (Düsseldorf: Econ, 1994), 11.

40. H.H. von Arnim, *Staat ohne Diener. Was schert die Politiker das Wohl des Volkes?* (Munich: Kindler, 1993).

41. Bräuninger and Hasenbeck, *Die Abzocker*, op. cit. 12.

42. Quoted by G. Eidam, *Unternehmen und Strafe. Vorsorge und Krisenmanagement* (Cologne: Carl Heymanns, 1993), vii.

neurotics in leadership positions.[43] Prominent philosophers discern a widening gap in our societies "between the stepped-up pace of scientific and technical developments and a stagnating or even regressive moral consciousness."[44] Because corporations are important initiators and motors of scientific-technological advances, they are in the direct line of fire when a society starts questioning the dependability of technology, the ability to calculate risks, and the reliability of science.

Among advocacy groups concerned with the problems of the developing world, the dominant perception is that corporations and their key executives have a more highly developed awareness of their rights than of their obligations. It is insinuated that they practice a "borderline morality," a term that G. Briefs defined in 1931 as the (lowest) level of morality that a society is prepared to recognize as just tolerable.[45] His presumption was that in a capitalistic system, business persons who are least constrained by moral scruples have the competitive advantage.

Many works on corporate ethics proceed implicitly or explicitly from the assumption that corporate morality is lower than that of other institutions, with the added inference that corporate higher-ups are morally lacking. In support of this assumption, authors refer over and again to the most widely cited public opinion polls.[46] Although these surveys prove little, lacking as they do the data that would allow methodologically sound comparisons with other institutions, they find broad public approval.

Many executives whose everyday experience gives them an altogether different slant cannot understand this mistrust. The numerous attempts to explain it all ring true in part, but none of them succeeds fully. For example, the blame for the public's negative opinion of business is often put on the mass media. And it is true that in the scramble to raise viewer

---

43. U. Beck, *Gegengifte. Die organisierte Unverantwortlichkeit* (Frankfurt a.M.: Suhrkamp, 1988); J. Hesse and H.Ch. Schrader, *Die Neurosen der Chefs. Die seelischen Kosten der Karriere* (Frankfurt a.M.: Eichborn, 1994).

44. V. Hösle, *Die Krise der Gegenwart und die Verantwortung der Philosophie* (Munich: C.H. Beck, 1990), 23.

45. G. Briefs, "Sozialreform und Sozialgeist in der Gegenwart," in *Handwörterbuch der Soziologie* (1931),162. See also R. Lay, *Die Macht der Moral* (Düsseldorf: Econ, 1990), 206 ff.

46. Starting from R. Baumhart, "How ethical are Businessmen?" in *Harvard Business Review* vol. 39, no. 4 (1961): 6-19 and 157-176; St.N. Brenner and E.A. Molander, "Is the ethics of business changing?" in *Harvard Business Review* (Jan., Feb. 1977): 57-71; H. Becker and D.J. Fritzsche, "Business Ethics: A Cross-Cultural Comparison of Managers' Attitude," *Journal of Business Ethics* vol. 6, no. 4 (1987): 289-295.

ratings and circulation figures, the purportedly sleazy byways of company doings often get more coverage than the normal highways. It is also true that journalists who file positive or balanced accounts of what goes on in the corporate world are looked at askance by certain colleagues as "court reporters." Furthermore, a lot of media have a pervasive penchant for taking problems that have but the remotest connection with companies as a pretext to smear them. Seldom is a finely shaded and objective analysis of a problem area done.

Still, all this falls well short of accounting for the negative public attitude. It is also correct to point out that prejudices simply exist and that people who have no direct knowledge of corporate life tend, because they are unable to form their own judgment, to play it safe by expressing themselves skeptically in opinion polls. But if this were the entire explanation, then companies themselves could help to clear up the misconceptions by communicating better. Another attempt at explanation says that every institution that embodies "power" in one shape or another is generally viewed with disapproval nowadays, but this is at best only partly correct.

A survey of young people in Germany in the mid-1990s showed an extremely low degree of trust in institutions in general, but business institutions came off markedly worse than others. While 42 percent of those polled declared their "complete trust" in the Federal Constitutional Court, only 29 percent felt the same about banks and just 20 percent about businesses.[47] From the business point of view, there is scant consolation to be drawn from the fact that the Federal Government and the Bundestag (lower house)—at 21 percent and 18 percent, respectively—did not come out well either.

As a final perhaps trivial and yet noteworthy indication of how overshadowed with skepticism the public standing of managers has become, we can cite the negative picture of them painted in films and fiction: rapacious scoundrels who stop at nothing, and at no matter what cost to the health and life of others, in order to feather their own nests foremost, but also to enrich their firms. True, with an eye to what sells, these books, films, and articles in newsweeklies and TV magazines may crassly overdo the reality. But for the consuming public, they only confirm the folk wisdom that where there's smoke, there's fire.

The loss of moral standing that business institutions have suffered is

47. Alfred Herrhausen Society for International Dialogue (ed.), *Jugend und Gesellschaft* (Frankfurt a.M., 1994), 38.

too pronounced to be explained away as due to some prevailing wind of anti-authoritarianism. The skepticism is also evident among those who are more knowledgeable and have a better understanding of the workings of business. Students of business management, for example, are critical of the exclusive concentration on short-term, purely quantitative goals that misleads managers into rejecting the qualitative aspects of business activity as "irrelevant." Management's perception of itself in this regard is also anything but unproblematic.

Members of top management appear to take a more positive view of the moral shape their companies are in. For most of them, often all's right with the world. Given that identification with "the company" grows stronger the higher up in the hierarchy a person is, this is not surprising. This should not lead to the conclusion that top management is also higher up morally, however. There are two possible explanations of why people at the top tend not to perceive any ethical problems: either moral predicaments are passed back down the line, or else blind spots or lost contact with reality have affected their power of sight.

In every survey aimed at soliciting managers' opinions, it has to be taken into account that the moral quality of their business in life could be higher in their own estimation than in that of others. Whenever both viewpoints have been probed and compared, notable divergences have shown up. It is also interesting that the causes of eroding corporate moral standards are in most cases ascribed to "outside" circumstances—a general decline in public morals, market pressures, corrupt politicians, and so on. At the same time, though, people discern plausible possibilities of improvement within the company.

Skeptical self-appraisal on the part of business leaders is not new. Some 20 years ago, Brenner and Molander published a study showing that 43 percent of the executives questioned felt themselves forced to resort to practices that they personally disapproved of morally but held to be necessary in order not to hazard the success of their company, and with it their own careers.[48] One reason behind this sadly schizophrenic state of mind, according to the American study, is a system of performance appraisal based almost solely on the criterion of short-term results. In addition, the study found most of the inducements reward primarily quickfix cost-cutting, sales-boosting, and profit-increasing measures without regard to long-term social and other repercussions.

---

48. St. N. Brenner and E. A. Molander, "Is the ethics of business changing?" in Ulrich and U. Thielemann (eds.), *Ethik und Erfolg. Unternehmensethische Denkmuster von Führungskräften-Eine empirische Studie* (Bern, Stuttgart, Vienna: Paul Haupt, 1992), 57-71.

In the early 1980s, Robert Jackall found a widespread belief among managers that the end justifies all means and that those who repeatedly fail to "meet their targets" can kiss a career good-bye. This slant, said Jackall, shapes not only the behavior of the cadre but, in time, the company's moral consciousness.[49] Until quite recently, a concentration on short-term results and a favoring of shareholders as by far the most important stakeholders were more pronounced in U.S. than in European firms. As late as the early 1980s, European managers showed a stronger concern for the welfare of employees than did their U.S. colleagues and tended to be oriented more toward the long-term interest of their firms. But European publications also point to the existence of moral conflicts among managers, intimating that many of them feel at least some of the decisions they make amount to a heads-or-tails choice.

Surveys carried out in both industrial and developing countries bring out the perception that "in former times" the moral standards of business conduct were higher than they are today.[50] Whether this is fact or whether it is because people have come to expect more of business than just "doing business" and because critical voices have grown accordingly louder cannot be stated with certainty. What is clear is that polarity between the drive for profit and accountability to society at large will persist. One indicator of this is the ongoing debate in Germany and Switzerland over the contentious issue of shareholder value.

Still, the public's skeptical attitude should be alarming for corporations and those who direct their fortunes: people are not about to vouchsafe freedom of action to institutions they mistrust. On the contrary, they seek to bring them under control. But this, the leading circles of the economy in every country are unanimously convinced, runs counter to sustained business. Over the past two decades, business misconduct has put the existence of entire companies at risk. Thousands of employees of the companies affected have lost their jobs, and the confidence of broad sections of society in the viability of the market economy—and in the integrity and quality of politicians and executives as well—has been shaken for a long time to come. The free rein given at

---

49. R. Jackall, "Moral Mazes. Bureaucrazy and Managerial Work," in *Harvard Business Review* (September, October 1983): 118-130.
50. See P. Ulrich and U. Thielemann, *Ethik und Erfolg. Unternehmensethische Denkmuster von Führungskräften—Eine empirische Studie* (Bern, Stuttgart, Vienna: Paul Haupt, 1992); St.N. Brenner and E.A. Molander, "Is the ethics of business changing?" loc. cit. 57-71; see also McFeely, Wackerle and Jett, *Survey on Ethics: Results* (New York 1987).

times to the Manchester capitalism mentality in the new federal states following reunification is not suited to boosting people's trust in the market economy and the institutions that are its pillars.

If the moral level of firms in a highly developed industrial nation with its thicket of rules and regulations proves so questionable, what are we to expect of those doing business in developing countries, with their institutional shortcomings and dearth of sound governance?

6. Stakeholder Relations

In a rapidly globalizing, knowledge-based economy, sources of value creation in business are shifting from tangible assets such as land and equipment, to intangibles such as intellectual, human and social capital. While the relative importance of various assets is open to debate, we believe that relationships between a firm, its employees and other stakeholders constitute an important and yet undervalued business asset. However, in any pluralistic society, different stakeholders will give different answers when asked what standards of corporate activity need to be met in order for ethical demands to be satisfied. This is due to the differing interests of, for example, employees (concerned about income, job security, or working atmosphere), customers (product quality, price, safety, and innovation), suppliers (guarantees of demand, reasonable prices, and stable relations), the state (taxes and infrastructure), shareholders (share price and future expectations), the media (accurate, topical, and relevant information and background), environmental groups, people concerned about development, and others.

No company is an autonomous cosmos unto itself. In a process of ongoing interaction, business enterprises influence the world around them and are influenced in turn by the world. In pluralistic societies, it is entirely normal that there is a variety of values, views of the world, and interests. This competition can give rise to conflicts. If a company wants to be "liked," it must first and foremost avoid antipathy—to achieve this, it must develop empathy. It therefore has to open up and address demands made on it by external stakeholders.

German philosopher Jürgen Habermas, the father of modern stakeholder theories, proposed in his approach to solving problems by communication that all controversial issues should be decided in dominance free discourse between all who have a stake in the issue on the basis of arguments that are likely to lead to a consensus.[51] The requirement of "dominance-free communication" describes the (ideal-typical) situation in which all parties involved have symmetrical opportunities to express themselves rather than one of an "authority"-versus "subject" attempt to assert claims to the "truth."[52] Dominance free communication also includes the timely exchange of information to ensure that all parties are working within the same framework of knowledge.

Habermas assumes that the societal validity of any standards in the long term depends on these standards being recognized and accepted as valid by all relevant stakeholders. In other words: what is of importance to all who are affected (or have a stake) cannot be decided by individual players.[53] Sustainable political changes deserve intersubjective recognition and acceptance. This makes monologue solutions impossible.

Since it is in the company's own interest to know and cultivate the societal environment that it perceives to be relevant, "stakeholder relations" today form a natural part of the management's responsibilities. There is a trade-off between a corporate position that is not at all investing in stakeholder relations and is consciously willing to run the risk of some criticism by some stakeholders and a corporate position that is actively looking for stakeholder dialogue. Our personal experience is that those who listen to others, take the concerns of others seriously, address the concerns, and themselves adopt clear positions become in the process part of a communicating community. And this is advantageous as it helps not only to know and come to terms with the way in which our own actions are seen by other members of civil society, but also to know the people behind the various stakeholder positions. Although even the

51. On the contribution of Jürgen Habermas to the ethics of discourse, see also J. Habermas, *Moralbewußtsein und kommunikatives Handeln*, 7th ed. (Frankfurt a.M.: Suhrkamp 1999); J. Habermas, *Theorie des kommunikativen Handelns*, 2 vols (Frankfurt a.M.: Suhrkamp, 1981); J. Habermas, *Erläuterungen zur Diskursethik* (Frankfurt a.M.: Suhrkamp, 1991); and J. Habermas, *Faktizität und Geltung. Beiträge zur Diskurstheorie des Rechts und des demokratischen Rechtsstaats* (Frankfurt a.M.: Suhrkamp, 1992); as well as J. Habermas, *Die Einbeziehung des Anderen. Studien zur politischen Theorie* (Frankfurt a.M.: Suhrkamp, 1999). On the debate surrounding this construct of ideas, see J.-P. Harpes and W. Kuhlmann (eds.), *Zur Relevanz der Diskursethik. Anwendungsprobleme der Diskursethik in Wirtschaft und Politik* (Münster: IT Verlag, 1997).
52. J. Habermas and N. Luhmann, *Theorie der Gesellschaft und Sozialtechnologie* (Frankfurt a.M.: Suhrkamp, 1971), 137 ff. On the degeneration of communication, see also R. Lay, *Kommunikation für Manager* (Düsseldorf: Econ Verlag 1989), 113 ff.
53. J. Habermas, *Moralbewußtsein und kommunikatives Handeln*, 7th ed. (Frankfurt a.M.: Suhrkamp, 1999), 75.

most enlightened company can never be equally receptive to all stakeholder groups, it is in the enlightened self-interest of the company to know what claims who is making with what legitimacy. The remark by Martin Buber that "through the 'Thou', a man becomes 'I'" applies in a modified form also to companies: they establish their identity in the way they deal with their societal environment.

Only a sober professional analysis allows meaningful conclusions to be drawn as to the validity of claims made on the company by outside stakeholder groups. Dissent on essential aspects needs to be accepted as a "rule of the game"—in the hope that unorthodox thinking also offers the opportunities to find innovative solutions. Evasive strategies (such as "sitting out" conflicts), ideological explanations for a rejection, or a self-prescribed unwillingness to compromise will leave a company out in the cold and vulnerable to unpleasant surprises. The very fact that a company delegates people to enter into a dialogue with stakeholder groups in order to present its own positions, to respond rationally to counterarguments, and to listen in turn to the other side keeps a company from sinking into the kind of anonymity that is so often the cause of diffuse feelings of disquiet and unease. (See also Chapter 15.)

There is a professional consensus that a number of principles and procedures have proved useful for companies with international operations:

- Acknowledgment of the fact that the societal environment as a whole, and especially those parts of civil society directly affected by the activities of a company, has a legitimate entitlement to have interests taken into account; at the very least, any restrictions, impositions, or even damage must be kept to a minimum, and ideally positive externalities should be maximized.
- A framework for communication with all the relevant stakeholder groups of the company.
- Ongoing sciences-based analysis of the arguments of all relevant stakeholders on all aspects that are important in terms of the corporate strategy and sustainable development of the company.
- Ongoing evaluation of the potential implications of these arguments for the corporate strategy and future success of the company as well as the need for strategic adaptations.
- Ongoing communication with all relevant stakeholder groups of the company, including the shareholders—"ongoing" is taken here to mean explicitly that communication is important not only in problematical times and in public conflicts and controversies, but at

all times regardless of any such conflict situations. This puts a company in the position of conveying complex internal realities to the outside world and external perceptions of strategically important facts (risks, benefits, fears, vulnerabilities) to the internal organization. Communication that embraces the fact that there are potential conflicts between the interests of the company and those of outside stakeholders and that there are dilemma situations for which there is no resolution in the sense of a solution that is satisfactory for everyone.

Such a corporate communications strategy is neither new nor revolutionary: Most companies do precisely this on their "product markets": companies examine the latest product developments, test the developments of the competition in the light of their own progress, and draw conclusions in order to gain optimum competitive advantage. The same professional approach to different kinds of evaluation, demands, and changes in *zeitgeist* on the "opinion markets" has a similar objective: a review of the ongoing development in the company's positions on the "opinion and evaluation markets" in competition with social stakeholders who engage in social assessments of the legitimacy of corporate action. The most successful possible competition on the "opinion markets" ultimately has a major influence on the way the company is perceived by society and thus on the company's success in the "product markets." Such an approach has a number of advantages for the company.

Anyone who remains in constant touch with the changing demands of the *zeitgeist* is in the picture much earlier and has a better chance of not suffering any "unpleasant" surprises. Most controversial and hotly debated issues in society that have led to substantial problems for exposed companies already formed a part of the scientific disputes that prevailed for years beforehand and subsequently became part of the work of specialized stakeholders. This is best illustrated by the development of the ecological debate: if the global corporate world had addressed the issues of environmental protection as openly and constructively in the late 1970s as it did many years later in preparation for the UN Conference on Environment and Development in 1992, a much faster social learning process would have been possible—to the benefit of future generations. It is in the nature of the issue that not all demands from "outside" are ultimately considered legitimate from the point of view of the company. By giving serious consideration to stakeholder demands and coming to grips with different kinds of value systems, a company can also help itself to anticipate changes in society's constellation of values. Companies that—by virtue of their stakeholder relations—were aware of the move to apply economic and social rights to business enterprises had more time to prepare themselves and react in a more professional way.

And a further point would appear to be clear as well: companies cannot solve all problems alone, but only in coalition with other partners of goodwill. It would be of no help to the company to be depicted as an unscrupulous, money-grubbing organization with no interest in HIV/AIDS patients—and it would be of no help to future patients of poverty-related diseases if, as a result of public pressure on prices, the pharmaceutical industry withdrew from R&D on medicines to treat such diseases. The demand for access to life-saving medicines is in all events a legitimate one. The question that remains to be answered, however, is to whom the demand for social sharing of responsibilities and possible coalitions of reason should be addressed—in addition to the pharmaceutical industry.

Given that a major part of modern societies today has much more trust in NGOs such as Amnesty International or Greenpeace than in political institutions or companies, clearly the "political process" has become more complex. Companies that are especially affected in their degree of freedom by general or sociopolitical factors are therefore well advised to do their "homework" also in these political terms. The question of whether a company's outside stakeholders have moral legitimacy has long since been answered, and the response is clearly affirmative.

Addressing the arguments of outside stakeholders means coming to terms not only with the content of the arguments but also with the human aspect of the debate. Dialogue takes place between people, not between institutions. We have known since Socrates that people tend to mistake their subjective beliefs for the objective truth. This confusion of subjective beliefs and objective truth, which has an inter-subjective value because it excludes error and deception, is often the cause of all evil.

Knowing the people behind the arguments improves the chances of understanding their thinking. In the best-case scenario, a learning process takes place that leads to qualitatively better solutions without a public showdown. The idealized assumption is made here that both parties involved are able to accept the power of the better argument.

7. Ethics and Morality in an Age of Globalization

Globalization—the totality of many complex social, economic, political, and cultural processes and interactions—seems to have been a mixed blessing and therefore continues to trigger a highly polarized discussion. It can be seen as the latest stage in the development of capitalism—or, in a less ideological way, as the result of improved and less expensive transportation and communication means. The corresponding reflexes it tends to trigger from proponents and opponents alike are therefore not altogether surprising: For some, the liberated flow of capital, goods, services, and ideas opens up immense opportunities of employment, income, and wealth. For others, it fosters the relative, if not absolute, impoverishment of whole groups of countries and the majority of their inhabitants.

A recent analysis from globalization opponents can be summarized as showing that globalization policies have contributed to increased poverty, greater inequality between and within nations, more widespread hunger, increased corporate concentration, reduced social services, and decreased power of labor vis-à-vis global corporations.[54] Where advocates of economic globalization see a window of opportunity through the consistent and efficient use of comparative advantages (in wage costs, for example, or the density of state regulations), opponents fear that globalization will set in motion a downward social and ecological spiral and an erosion of state sovereignty to the detriment of the common good. The hopes for the blessings that a convergence of economic and finance policy will bring and the wish for economic integration are contrasted with fears that traditional social safety nets will be destroyed and with warnings of the widening gap in income and wealth.

The general tenor of these voices is that globalization goes hand in hand with an intellectual hegemony of western origin and an imposed change of values. While there are those who praise this change because they see it as leading to greater efficiency and productivity, others denounce it because they fear it will lead to "predatory capitalism" on a global level, with all its unsavory features such as greed, ruthlessness, and egoism.[55] Most opponents claim that economic globalization lacks an ethical framework and political underpinnings (if not control) to ensure

---

54. D. Barker and J. Mander (eds.), *Does Globalization Help the Poor?* International Forum on Globalization (San Francisco 2001); see also D.C. Korten, *Globalizing Civil Society. Reclaiming our Right to Power* (New York: Seven Stories Press, 1998).

55. The term "predatory capitalism" was introduced by Noam Chomsky in 1973; see N. Chomsky, *For Reasons of State*, (New York: Pantheon, 1973), 403f.

that economic performance is subordinated to essential human and social goals. The perception that globalization has shifted power away from governments and toward the private sector, in particular toward multinational corporations, is widespread—and sets off fears of abuse and consequently leads to calls for international legal standards in addition to voluntary codes delineating the practices of corporate social responsibility.

Disagreement also prevails as to the empirically measurable effects. Whereas there are those who point to the association between an open world market and economic growth and suggest that with a "growing pie" all the distribution problems will be easier to solve, others point out not only that this is by no means automatic, but also that the tendency actually goes in the opposite direction. In their view, economic globalization is likely to precipitate a return to a type of global Manchester capitalism: workers for their wages and governments with their regulation and tax levels in one poor country must compete ever more fiercely with workers and governments in other poor countries. This, they fear, will lead to the worldwide erosion of social and environmental standards, to more marked social asymmetries and even the re-proletarianization of labor, and to permanent damage to the environment.

Since the empirically measurable effects are seen to be so controversial, there is also no clearcut answer to the essential question of whether globalization-induced social disparities or faults are inevitable problems of the transition and thus the net balance will be positive within an "acceptable period"—or whether the opposite is the case. Generally, say the skeptics, there is "no overall tedency for the poorer countries to catch up or converge with richer countries."[56] Indeed, it appears to have become the new conventional wisdom that globalization has increased inequality between and within nations and will continue to do so. Not so, counter the proponents of globalization, who draw on their own statistics to show that the very opposite is the case: "So far, the current wave of globalization, which started around 1980, has actually promoted economic equality and reduced poverty."[57]

It was the Stoic philosopher Epiktet who more than 2,000 years ago drew attention to the fact that "people are not bothered by facts, but by

---

56. J. Sachs and A. Warner, "Economic Reform and the Process of Global Integration," in *Brookings Papers on Economic Activity*, no. 1 (Washington, D.C., 1995): 1-118.

57. See D. Dollar and A. Kraay, "Spreading the Wealth," in *Foreign Affairs*, vol. 81, no. 1 (2002): 120-133.

their perception of facts." And—not the least due to a predominantly negative reporting—the public perception of globalization is currently negative. Evaluating the enormous number of critical publications, the press coverage on the subject, and even more the tenor of demonstrations in the streets of Porto Allegre, Genoa, Prague, or Seattle, the consequences of globalization are widely perceived to threaten just about all valuable political and social achievements of the past 100 years—be it democracy, human rights, workers' rights, sustainable management of the environment, or others. Even icons of international finance such as George Soros and former World Bank chief economist and Nobel laureate Joseph E. Stiglitz—for many years part of the "usual suspects" crowd—have gone on record expressing discontent and criticism.[58]

We agree with the enlightened judgment of Paul Streeten as well as the wisdom of his quote of the Grand Old Lady of economic theory, Joan Robinson:

> "Joan Robinson said that there is only one thing that is worse than being exploited by capitalists, and that is not being exploited by them. The same goes for participation in globalization. Those with skills and assets take advantage of the opening up to globalization; those without them get left behind. But there are better options than to allow these people to become the victims of the blind forces of globalization. Measures such as social safety nets, guaranteed employment schemes and training provisions to cushion poor people in low-income countries against being battered by these forces should be built into the system of international relations. This is necessary not only for political stability, but for reasons of our common humanity."[59]

A constructive contribution toward these goals of political stability and humanity must also be expected from the private sector—and in particular from multinational corporations, which have been the main agents of globalization. In addition to global consumers (who got more choice and better prices), these companies benefited the most from the advantages of moving financial and intellectual capital, new technologies, and efficient organizational skills between different nations. National

---

58. G. Soros, *On Globalization*, (New York: Public Affairs, 2002); J. Stiglitz, *Die Schatten der Globalisierung* (Munich: Siedler, 2002 (*Globalizaton and its Discontents*, Allen Lane / The Penguin Press, 2002).

59. P. Streeten, *Globalization: Threat or Opportuity* (Copenhagen: Copenhagen Business School Press, Handelsshojlens Forlag, 2001), 33.

governments and work forces did not and do not enjoy such mobility. In principle they can invest and divest in alternative countries according to the best socio-economic and institutional framework offered. This mobility-induced distribution of power, according to the critics, makes such corporations unaccountable and is misused to play potential host countries off against one another for their investments in a competition for the lowest possible pay, social security contributions, and taxes as well as the laxest environmental protection laws. This perception is underpinned at least on a case-by-case basis by reports of multinational companies being involved in abusing and exploiting workers and causing harm to the environment.[60]

This at least partly explains why—in addition to uneasiness with free trade, deregulation, and the spread of some modern technologies— transnational corporations are the focus of skepticism if not outright societal distrust. According to recent polls in countries that belong to the OECD, NGOs such as Amnesty International, Greenpeace, or Oxfam— many of them at least to some extent critical of transnational corporations and globalization—enjoy substantially more trust in affluent societies than corporations with global operations. When asked, "Which institutions operate in the best interest of society?" 65 percent of respondents named NGOs and only 42 percent pointed to "global companies."[61]

Needless to say, negative opinion on multinational corporations is also contrasted with other, more positive reports, but these have attracted little attention. In cases where companies with international operations transferred production abroad, the effects in recipient countries have generally been favorable. The 1994 *World Investment Report* described transnationals as the main vehicle for the achievement of economic stability and prosperity in developing nations, as they stimulated economic growth and improved the recipient countries' international competitiveness.[62] Many companies are today aware of the fact that the perception of their social and ecological performance acts as a societal

---

60. See *Corporate Watch* (www.corpwatch.org), *Multinational Monitor*, or *Corporate Crime Reporter* (P.O. Box 18384, Washington, DC 20036, (www.essential.org, www.globalexchange.org); also P.S. Sethi, "Human Rights and Corporate Sense," in *Far Eastern Economic Review* (October 19, 2001): 37; and "Global Capitalism: Can it be made to work better?" in *Business Week* (November 6, 2000): 72-90.

61. See Edelman *Public Relations World Wide* (November 2001), for similar attitudes; see also Environics, *The Millenium Poll* (New York, 1999); also MORI, *Annual Business & the Environment study* (London 2000).

62. United Nations, *World Investment Report. Transnational Corporations, Employment and the Workplace* (New York/Geneva, 1994).

"license to operate," affecting the level of freedom that their enterprise enjoys. This is especially true for companies whose innovative products and services are subject to government regulation. These companies endeavor out of enlightened self-interest to be successful not only in the marketplace, where they sell their products, but also in the "market" of public and political opinion. However, the perception of a single player always depends on the reputation of the whole industrial sector—and this is often colored by the occasional "black sheep." Since it is ultimately the performance of the weakest that shapes the overall perception of multinational corporations, there should be more pressure from within the private sector to accelerate changes for the better and to prevent corporate worst-cases of social and ecological responsibility. There is no excuse for corporate misconduct—this should be made clear not only from the critic's side.

NGOs and the media (rightly) pick up blatant misconduct. Today's power and sophistication of the media provide important ways of influencing how people think and what they believe to be true. The worst cases of corporate misconduct attract media and hence public attention and get stored in collective memories. As cognitive theory tells us, these stored memories contribute to the construction of individual perceptions of reality: what people perceive as their "objective" reality is predetermined by each individual's experience (stored memories), value systems, views of the future, and other influences. Our perception of reality therefore depends not just on what occurs in our social environment but also inevitably on how we apprehend this "what." What is taken by an individual to be the clearly perceptible "objective" reality is conditioned by the subjective manner in which we seek "our" reality. Information is selected, evaluated, and classified, and anything that does not bear subjective inspection is not admitted to the judgment forming process. Bad news has a tendency to attract more attention than good news. Good news, especially if communicated by the corporations themselves, is often perceived to be the result of corporate propaganda efforts and therefore assumed to be biased.

Naturally, the effects of a phenomenon as complex as globalization are not exclusively beneficial. As with any social change, there are risks as well as benefits, both winners and losers—not only in the South, but also in the North. Low-skilled workers in Europe, for example, have many reasons to perceive the economic development of many countries in the South as a threat to them, which could be one reason for the rising popularity of rightwing parties. Southern countries that saw their industries suddenly unprepared and needlessly exposed to international competition faced immense problems with high social costs and preventable damage for many people. For southern countries, it is fair to say, the policy variables in the architecture of international finance, the structural policies of industrial countries, and the extent and quality of international development aid all have a major influence on the institutional capacity to deal with globalization. Reform proposals, such as those made for the International Monetary Fund or the World Bank, are therefore important. In addition, it is difficult to comprehend that many of those in the North who go on record as advocates of free trade introduce tariffs, non-tariff restrictions, and subsidies to limit imports from the developing world. Such policies deprive the developing world of the trade-income opportunities they badly need to finance their social development endeavors.

Having said this, it is important to draw attention to the national responsibilities to enable countries to better cope with the effects of globalization. The ratio of benefits to risks—and hence of winners to losers—depends to a large extent on national political and social parameters such as the quality of education and skills. Particular emphasis here is placed on the general extent to which the ideal of "good governance" is put into practice. As noted by the Commission on Global Governance:

> "Governance is the sum of the many ways individuals and institutions, public and private, manage their common affairs. It is the continuing process through which conflicting or diverse interests may be accommodated and co-operative action may be taken. It includes formal institutions and regimes empowered to enforce compliance, as well as informal arrangements that people and institutions either have agreed to or perceive to be in their interest." [63]

In this context, general political quality variables such as peaceful settlements of disputes, democracy and legitimacy, justice and equity, and the rule of the law or transparency and accountability are as important as such political and social subparameters as the level of regulation, the taxation system, or the quality of social or competition policy. Precisely in these times of globalization, therefore, the calls for developing as well as industrial countries to get their house in order in this respect have lost none of their justification.

---

63. Commisssion on Global Governance, *Our Global Neighbourhood* (Oxford University Press 1995), 2.

Whatever other players have to assume in the way of duties, it is just as clear that the social and ecological quality of commitment on the part of the main players in globalization—namely, the multinational companies—can and should make a significant difference. Those who have more resources at their disposal in terms of finance, technology, and knowledge also have a greater responsibility for the common good. On no account would it be legitimate to exploit the absence of appropriate legislation or credible regulatory controls for the infringement of labor rights and pollution of the environment. Especially for developing countries, with their potential lack of resources for state-of-the-art legislation and verification, we have to remind ourselves that not everything that is legal is also legitimate. Legality is often only the ethical minimum. Therefore, where the national standards are inadequate or enforcement not credible, the company would be expected to set and enforce its own—higher—standards.

Not only is this "the right thing to do," a responsible attitude of this kind is in the enlightened self-interest of all players in civil society. Globalization as an economic, social, and ecological process will only succeed and gain societal acceptance if and when its overall balance sheet is positive on a broad social base. It would be the most dangerous form of self-deception to assume that without explicit commitments to this end globalization would produce an undifferentiated "positive" outcome.

Since there are no easy and certainly no quick solutions to complicated problems, only two things can be recommended in the current context:

- Blatant corporate misconduct must be publicly condemned: whenever worst cases become known from one company, all other companies and the acceptance of the globalization process suffer by association. In addition, all efforts should be supported through which the private sector can make tangible contributions that help create a higher level of compliance with human rights and enhance the quality of social and environmental affairs.
- As globalization results in more interdependence and as interdependence requires more cooperation, all parties working in good faith for sustainable development must not only communicate on an equal footing and engage with other peoples' perceptions but also, inspired by the ethics of responsibility, search for ways to achieve a pragmatic consensus in the interests of all parties.

These two recommendations are the minimum preconditions to start a multi-stakeholder effort that could lead us away from the current polarization.

PART II

TRUSTEES OF MORALITY

Even today many people still hold to the view that a corporate ethic is superfluous: the market and the law suffice as "trustees of morality," they claim. They argue that the free interaction of all participants in the economic process is the sole guarantor of the public welfare and that no more is needed than respect for the laws in force. Chapters 8 and 9 argue, in contrast, that—by themselves—neither the market nor the law necessarily involve the due consideration for social and ecological concerns that is morally called for.

Chapter 10 goes into the question of whether businesses as institutions and the people in them should act as trustees of morality— and if so, under which institutional premises or corporate culture aegis. The point is made that corporate creativity shaped by principles of reason can founder on various organizational barriers, and that in the end it is people who must overcome them.

Chapter 11 looks at a new tool in efforts to improve the state of global responsibility—the UN Global Compact proposed by Secretary-General Kofi Annan in January 1999. The chapter considers the pluses and minuses of companies signing on to the Compact, and discusses why companies should join this international effort to bring universal values into global markets and corporate practices.

8. The Market as Trustee of Morality

*The natural effort of every individual to better his own
condition, when suffered to exert itself with freedom and
security, is so powerful a principle, that it is alone, and
without any assistance, not only capable of carrying on
the society to wealth and prosperity, but of surmounting
a hundred impertinent obstructions with which the folly
of human laws too often encumbers its operations;
though the effect of these obstructions is always more or
less either to encroach upon its freedom, or to diminish
its security.*

Adam Smith[1]

In 1776 Adam Smith published his most famous work, *An Inquiry into
the Nature and Causes of the Wealth of Nations*, as a theoretical defense
of individualism in contrast to all medieval and mercantilist concepts of
society and of the material prosperity of these individuals, depictable in
terms of money but not necessarily consisting of that.[2] Economic
liberalism, which found its classic proponent in Smith, is a salient facet of
the broad liberal movement that began in seventeenth-century England
as a vigorous protest against the theory and practice of the omnipotent
state. It aimed to draw a strict line between the state and the individual.
This explains why its appearance coincided with that of modern theories
of natural rights that, in deriving the state from the individual, place
government in the service of individual interest. Classical economic
liberalism flatly rejects the interventionism that typifies mercantilism. It
holds artificial constraints on production, as embodied by the guild
system, to fetter progress as much as customs barriers between nations
do. Freedom of trade and industry thus figures as the most important
postulate of early economic liberalism.

For Adam Smith, the foundations of a people's prosperity were
diligence and thrift. He took it for granted that under conditions of free
competition people would learn and practice these traits out of self-
interest. He also presumed that people were impelled by mutual goodwill and that their human nature and therefore their needs were largely
the same. In a climate of freedom, this would lead to a balanced
apportionment of goods. The free interplay of supply and demand would
of necessity bring about pricing in line with production costs, thus

---

1.   Adam Smith, *An Inquiry into the Nature and Causes of the Wealth of Nations* (New
   York: Modern Library, 1937), 508.

2.   Ibid.

serving the consumer's interest. The market regulates the workings of the economy as if by the agency of "invisible hands."

Even today, respectable economists and industrialists are convinced that the market economy suffices, in the sense of ordered competitive performance and respect of the law, to do justice to the principle of the general welfare.[3] Competition induces materially optimal performance and in so doing brings forth the highest possible benefits to the general welfare. Economists of this school take individual self-interest as their point of departure, which in their view requires no ethical justification since the result of ordered competition—namely, economic growth— provides the justification. In other words, as Milton Friedman put it, "the business of business is business"—and this is adequate to define the role assigned to companies in the division of labor in a society. To be sure, social and ethical considerations certainly play a part in the business decision-making process, but only insofar as they are made manifest by customers and public opinion and in the laws. When a company behaves unsuitably, society reacts negatively. Since business people want in their own best interest to avoid this, their conduct—so goes the logic—will be beyond moral reproach.

There does in fact appear to exist something like a "moralizing force" of the market. We need only call to mind the protests and boycotts launched by consumer advocacy organizations and churches, the negative reporting in the media, the demonstrations at factory gates. Because vehement criticism from outside is at a minimum damaging to a company's image, puts management on the defensive, and may even result in palpable sales losses, simple prudence dictates that a company refrain from doing things that stir up adverse public reactions. For all that, however, the market's "invisible hand" is still not strong enough to qualify as the guardian of morality, for where social and ecological matters are concerned, the market is largely blind.

The Misunderstood Adam Smith

When Adam Smith states that "It is not from the benevolence of the butcher, the brewer, or the baker, that we expect our dinner, but from their regard to their own interest," we can readily assent.[4] However, when

---

3. The two most well-known are probably Peter Drucker and Milton Friedman. See Peter Drucker, "What is Business Ethics?" in *The Public Interest* vol. 63 (1981): 18- 36; Milton Friedman, "The Social Responsibility of Business to Increase its Profits," in *The New York Times Magazine* (September 13, 1970): 32 f, and 122-126; —, *Kapitalismus und Freiheit* (Stuttgart: Seewald Verlag, 1971).
4. Adam Smith, op cit. 14.

the proponents of the market economy base their case on this self-interest hypothesis—and when, conversely, its opponents condemn Smith on that account—a grave misunderstanding arises. His work seems to have become the hapless victim of a vicious circle of indirect quotation. Few authors seem to take the trouble to actually read his works anymore in their full original version; instead, all manners of interpretations are taken over from secondary sources and run through the critical mill.

Adam Smith, it is true, did consider self-interest to be the central element of economic progress and prosperity; but at the same time he was a fervent critic of self-interest as the sole basic motive force driving human behavior. His vision of human nature was far removed from the naively romantic construct commonly imputed to him. He was a moral philosopher, and precisely as such he was quite familiar with human moral frailty. The man who appealed to magnanimity, humanity, goodness, compassion, mutual friendship, and respect was also aware of the existence of the hard and adamant heart that, feeling only for itself, is completely oblivious to the happiness or misery of others.[5] Thus he says, for example:

> "Commerce, which ought naturally to be, among nations, as
> among individuals, a bond of union and friendship, has become
> the most fertile source of discord and animosity. The capricious
> ambition of kings and ministers has not…been more fatal to the
> repose of Europe, than the impertinent jealousy of merchants and
> manufacturers. The violence and injustice of the rulers of
> mankind is an ancient evil, for which, I am afraid, the nature of
> human affairs can scarce admit of a remedy. But the mean ra-
> pacity, the monopolizing spirit of merchants and manufacturers,
> who neither are, nor ought to be, the rulers of mankind, though it
> cannot perhaps be corrected, may very easily be prevented from
> disturbing the tranquility of any body but themselves."[6]

Smith holds "merchants and manufacturers" to account for the doubts cast on the free market economy; their "interested sophistry [has] confounded the common sense of mankind."[7] He saw "mercantile envy," leading as it does to the formation of commercial power groups that

---

5.   Adam Smith, *The Theory of Moral Sentiments* (London 1853, New York 1966), 47-49.
6.   Adam Smith, *An Inquiry into the Nature and Causes of the Wealth of Nations,* op. cit. 460.
7.   Ibid. 461.

impair the effective working of orderly competition, as the real wrecker of the market economy's functional mechanisms and foundations.

Further, Smith berates those establishments that, quite legally, paid their workers only subsistence-level wages, as well as the guild regulations that made it difficult for exploited workers to change jobs.[8] And almost 100 years before the advent of Marxism and post-Marxist socialism, he pleads in favor of securing the basic material needs of the working class:

> "Servants, laborers and workmen of different kinds, make up the far greater part of every great political society. But what improves the circumstances of the greater part can never be regarded as an inconvenience to the whole. No society can surely be flourishing and happy, of which the far greater parts of the members are poor and miserable. It is but equity, besides, that they who feed, cloth and lodge the whole body of the people, should have such a share of the produce of their own labor as to be themselves tolerably well fed, clothed and lodged."[9]

And:

> "The liberal reward of labor...increases the industry of the common people...which, like every other human quality, improves in proportion to the encouragement it receives. A plentiful subsistence increases the bodily strength of the laborer, and the comfortable hope of bettering his condition, and of ending his days perhaps in ease and plenty, animates him to exert that strength to the utmost. Where wages are high, accordingly, we shall always find the workmen more active, diligent, and expeditious, than where they are low."[10]

The regard paid by Smith to a fair living wage was of great significance under the social conditions in England in his day and remains highly relevant for developing countries today. Even then he saw the connection between the high birth rates and high mortality rate that went hand in hand with poverty:

> "But one-half the children born, it is computed, die before the

---

8.   Ibid. 134 f.
9.   Ibid. 78-79.
10. Ibid. 81.

age of manhood. The poorest laborers, therefore...must, one with
another, attempt to rear at least four children, in order that two
may have an equal chance of living to that age."[11]

We fail to do Adam Smith justice, then, in claiming that he held high self-
interest to the exclusion of all else. Beyond self-interest he postulated
moral concepts that were and are applicable to the economy and
business. Not by chance was he named to the Chair of Moral Philosophy
in the University of Glasgow in 1752, 24 years before his magnum opus
appeared. And a few years after taking up professorship, in 1759, he
presented *The Theory of Moral Sentiments*, a standard treatise on ethics
years before the "Wealth of Nations."

Limits of the Market as Trustee of Morality

No doubt it is now generally recognized that a "free" market economy in
its ideal depiction is as unrealistic as the opposing model of a planned
economy. The general welfare does not amount to just the sum of
individual interests, nor, conversely, can the public interest be reduced
merely to the private interest.

The unalloyed market mechanism that ultra-liberals clamor for under
the banner of full-fledged "deregulation" is unsuccessful in coping with
social problems, notably unemployment. Often forgotten are those who,
for lack of purchasing power, are unable to participate in the market as
well as the unemployed who are in search of a job—unless, that is, a
jobless person manages to displace an employed person by working for
lower pay. The social costs that accrue from a high rate of unemployment
(social disintegration, decline in the level of education, deterioration of
moral values, substance abuse, and so on) are not internalized—that is,
they do not show up in the cost accounts of businesses, households, and
governments, or at least not to their full extent. Constructs like
"economically rational behavior" of all participants in the market, "total
transparency," "full-out competition," "expeditious adaptations," and so
on still belong more in the realm of theory than down-to-earth reality. In
particular, extreme differences in incomes and fortunes and the
monopoly-like power structure linked with them deviate conspicuously
from Smith's ideal of a moral political economy—most glaringly so in
developing countries.

The fact that the market does not work morally if its movers and

---

11. Ibid. 68.

makers are morally flawed also shows up in myriad instances of the self-interest mentality ruthlessly at work, riding roughshod over the health and lives of people. The greater the reach and potency of modern technology, the more devastating the effects of moral shortcomings in those who wield it. With mega-technology, the dimension of potential human error or negligence has expanded enormously. It will take longer to set right the consequences of short-term misdoing, as for example in dealing with nuclear waste or in running a nuclear power plant like Chernobyl, than has elapsed since the last Ice Age—quite apart from the irreversible human misery and incalculable harm already inflicted on the human and nonhuman gene pool.

In comparison with other systems, however, the competitively driven market economy is better suited to furthering economic efficiency, by virtue of which it contributes effectively to doing away with shortages. The moral and ecological aftereffects of the communist planned economy have been and continue to be too obvious to waste further comment on. There is no sensible alternative to a socially and ecologically compatible market economy—but blind trust in the self-regulating capacity of markets is just as misplaced as the hope that a strong state and an almighty bureaucracy can solve all problems.

9. The Law as Trustee of Morality

Otfried Höffe defines law as "the embodiment of normative obligations (norms, but also structures and procedures, together with the relevant modes of conduct) which—being valid at a certain time and for a certain political community—formally regulate societal life."[12] This broad definition encompasses legal norms, positive law, and societal norms. The law regulates who has to do what and demand what, and it also contains moral concepts such as "good faith," "good morals" or "manners." In this way the law contributes decisively, by way of commandments, prohibitions, and rules of behavior, to fixing the conditions that enable the members of a society to live together with a minimum of conflict. In addition, the law is always an effective means of discouraging or preventing criminal and culpably negligent behavior. To a substantial extent, the lawmaker thus also becomes the trustee of moral values.

---

12. See Otfried Höffe (ed.), *Lexikon der Ethik*, 3rd rev. ed. (Munich: Beck'sche Schwarze Reihe, vol. 152, 1986), s.v. "Recht," 202.

The Law of the Land and Its Interpretation

The lawmaker's trustee function has long been reinforced by High Court interpretations of the laws on the books. Where corporate ethics come into play, these pronouncements are of more than academic interest: they also have a direct impact on what a company does. One often cited example is the opinion handed down by the German Federal Court in the Erdal Case.[13] The point at issue concerned serious ailments, ranging from troubles in breathing to pulmonary edemas, that occurred in connection with leather sprays, even when used according to directions. As the reports kept multiplying, the management of the manufacturing firm decided on an internal investigation but not an end to marketing, let alone a product recall. The Erdal management's rationale: neither internal nor external chemical analysis had detected toxic properties in the suspect spray.

But the German Supreme Court upheld a federal court's decision that found the managing director guilty of negligent and willfully dangerous bodily injury. The judges rejected as inconsequential the argument that airtight scientific proof had been lacking. Although none of the members of management could be held blameworthy for not having initiated withdrawal of the product on his own, neither could any of them claim that the authority to do so was not within his (internally agreed) area of competence. On the contrary, "each of them was only obligated to exercise his power to act in full and to do everything possible and that might reasonably be expected of him in order to bring about a decision of company management to order and implement the necessary withdrawal."[14] This, however, they neglected to do.

In the leather spray case (1990), as in an earlier Contergan (thalidomide) lawsuit that ended in a product ban in December 1970, the court found unambiguously in favor of protecting the consumer over the economic defense offered by the company. This held good even if it afterwards turned out that a product withdrawal, with all the attendant administrative costs and sales losses, would not have been necessary. In the Contergan case, the judges specified several pointers to arriving at the requisite decisions and courses of action that, in case of doubt, could be considered "possible and reasonable."[15] From the perspective of corporate ethics, four are particularly relevant:

---

13.   See the article in *Frankfurter Allgemeine Zeitung*, no. 198 (August 27, 1990): 13.

14.   According to ibid.

15.   See J. Schmidt-Salzer, *Entscheidungssammlung Produkthaftung*, vol. II (Berlin 1979), 481 ff.

Judicious reasoning rather than final scientific proof... In weighing possible causal connections, "proof in the spirit of the law is definitely not to be equated with so-called scientific proof, which pre-supposes a mathematically precise certitude that rules out any other possibility. The sole decisive proof in judging whether or not an act is criminal...is based on a reasoned verdict that has taken into account all pertinent factors in the overall context of the matter at issue."[16]

...if there are grounds for suspicion. A serious reason to suspect that a product may have deleterious effects on health is sufficient to obligate its manufacturer to make this publicly known. In the Contergan case, the court found that adequate protection of the consumer was not ensured if the drug's manufacturer took protective measures only after its adverse side effects had been proved; "rather, in principle even a slight degree of suspicion is enough to require the manufacturer to take action."[17] Here, 22 years before the UN Conference on Environment and Development in Rio de Janeiro, the precautionary principle was established as binding on business conduct.

Objectivity, not "common practice". Nor in the judges' opinion can conclusions applicable to the "ought" status be extrapolated from the "is" status. Common practice in a branch of industry does not make a form of behavior lawful. "Customary practice in the industry does not define what is right and legitimate; the one decisive factor is the care which an objective review determines to be necessary."[18] With this ruling, argumentation to the effect that what someone has done, now a subject of dispute, is only something that "everyone" does becomes inoperative.

Conflicts of interest. In the Contergan case the court recognized an "unavoidable conflict of interest between the exigencies of scientific exactitude and the perfectly legitimate, economically even requisite, pursuit of profit." It also accepted (as later on in the Erdal case) that there are limits to the individual person's freedom to come to a decision. At the same time, the court noted that conflicts of interest and limited discretionary space do not exclude individual guilt by any means. Executives must have the courage to take a stand and to give steadfast personal commitment to ethically defensible decisions, even in the face of resistance in the responsible decision-making body:

---

16. Ibid. 485 f.
17. Ibid. 501 f and 505.
18. J. Schmidt-Salzer, *Entscheidungssammlung Produkthaftung*, vol. IV (München 1982), 280.

"Nor may personal difficulties be adduced as an excuse for not
taking decisive action. Considering the importance of
the...imminent danger of grave harm to health, they must if
necessary be expected to accept personal difficulties. This is not
to demand too much, since otherwise the health of many people
could be put at risk with impunity."[19]

The expectation that in case of doubt companies should subordinate
their business interests to higher, legally protected rights such as human
life and health or preservation of the environment is thus not only rooted
in ethical theory, it is also being increasingly sustained by judicial
opinions at the highest level.

Limits of the Law as Trustee of Morality

Almost a century ago Georg Jellinek made the point, in his *General Theory
of Political Science,* that the state cannot engender anything that belongs in
the domain of human inwardness alone.[20] The state can regulate the
externals of behavior, but it cannot induce a moral outlook. Through laws
it can only create a framework enabling people to develop ways of life that
in substance are quite independent of the state. Nor can it

"produce economic goods directly...It can only remove
impediments to economic activity and help to abet it...If the state
oversteps these, its natural boundaries, it can have but a
hampering or destructive effect. The essential productive
elements of a nation's whole culture therefore reside
predominantly in its individual people and in the part of society
not of the state."[21]

A person's moral conscience cannot be enacted, as it were; the law does
not relieve the individual of the onus of reflecting and practicing ethical
conduct. This being so, a nation's culture—with its fabric of morals,
manners, and values and its ideas of what constitutes a well-ordered
society—is not the product of a law-giving state. Rather, it is the culture
of a people that puts its stamp on the state. In a democratic country, after
all, the people choose who should represent them politically, so the

19. Ibid. 282.
20. G. Jellinek, *Das Recht des modernen Staates,* vol. 1, 2nd rev. ed., Allgemeine
     Staatslehre, (Berlin: O. Häring, 1905), 243.
21. Ibid. 244.

system of government can only be as perfect as those who stand for it. "Possession of power and enjoyment of legal protection cannot be the individual's highest purpose in life," Jellinek continues. "They are merely the preconditions for gaining and possessing other kinds of goods. In like fashion, with the upward movement of a culture new and higher fields of endeavor are opened up to the state."[22]

Legality and Morality

In his *Groundwork of the Metaphysic of Morals*, Immanuel Kant drew this distinction between the legality and the morality of an act:

> "Legality is defined in terms of whether or not an act, regardless of what motivates it, is in conformity with the law; whereas when the idea of obligation under the law is at the same time the motivating force, then this constitutes the morality of the act."[23]

Morality is "wanting-to-be-good become a staunch basic stance," or perceived responsibility issuing from better knowledge and better understanding, and it disallows taking advantage of gaps in the laws and misusing discretionary latitude to the detriment of other people, the environment, or posterity. Even against the backdrop of contemporary jurisprudence, Kant's distinction remains valid: not everything that is legal is also legitimate.

Legal Entitlements Have Certain Limits, While Ethical Claims Do Not

Law, as Gröschner puts it, is the "ordering of life relations in a grid of legal relations," which indicates its limited scope.[24] The law defines merely the ethical minimum. How minimal this is can be seen in the manifest inadequacy of the legal framework in many developing countries, for example, where as a result of institutional deficiencies or the existence of political violence the law is overridden. So even if the law does not expressly compel it, knowing better imposes the obligation to accept responsibility beyond the letter of the law.

---

22. Ibid. 250.
23. I. Kant, *Die Metaphysik der Sitten*, vol. VIII, 9th ed., W. Weischedel (ed.), (Frankfurt a.M.: Suhrkamp, 1991), 324.
24. R. Gröschner, "Zur rechtsphilosophischen Fundierung einer Unternehmensethik," in H. Steinmann and A. Löhr (eds.), *Unternehmensethik* (Stuttgart: C.E. Poeschel, 1989), 93-113.

Illustrations of how nominally law-abiding behavior falls short of preventing human suffering can be found in any newspaper archive. For example, some years ago a hotel in the Cairo suburb Heliopolis, part of an internationally well-known chain, burned down, leaving dead and wounded. The hotel had neither an alarm nor a sprinkler system. In response to reprimands from the international press, the management noted that in Egypt law did not require such installations. Yet notwithstanding this loop-hole, other hotels had installed the systems, so that the toll in the event of a comparable fire would in all likelihood be lower.

It need not always be a matter of life and death that dictates doing what is right and not just sticking to what is legal. Thus it would not be ethically acceptable for a multinational corporation operating in a developing country to orient its personnel policy on conditions sanctioned by the local laws if this meant, say, making 14-year-old children put in 10-hour days on the assembly line, dismissing women workers who became pregnant, or using unhealthy production processes forbidden in every industrial country.

Even when laws do exist, they often prove to have only limited effectiveness because someone who wants to overstep them weighs the possible minuses against the pluses to be gained from an infringement, calculating at the same time whether the probable advantage envisaged outweighs the chances of being caught. Where this pattern of calculating is regarded as "clever" business practice, the rules and regulations increasingly lose force. And when it even becomes possible, through corruption, to influence the intensity of the prosecution and the severity of the punishment, then the floodgates are flung wide open.

Over and above innumerable examples of the ineffectiveness of laws, there also exists a clear difference between juridical and ethical accountability. Whereas the juridical is contained within precisely defined bounds, a concern for the whole enjoins that ethical responsibility should not be equally confined. In an ethical perspective, not everything that is legal is desirable, and not everything that is desirable is a legal obligation.

Likewise with corporate ethics, we have to distinguish between legal obligation and moral obligation. Added to this is the fact that legislation is reactive, while morality works proactively. In most cases legislation does not anticipate how statutes can be circumvented but reacts instead to damage already done or to the types of individuals (often perceived as "clever" or "smart") who capitalize on loopholes. Since the institutional mills grind slowly, the reactions are often a long time coming. In many cases the laws do not result in overcoming what is wrong but instead merely shift it elsewhere.

Finally, and not least, we should recall that most corporations are "limited liability" companies. No business deliberately strives to go bankrupt. If this happens, however, it can quite legally file for bankruptcy, even if moral default on the part of management brought it about. The amount of compensation then mostly turns out to be far smaller than the actual damage that the company has wrought, since normally the private fortunes of those responsible cannot be touched. As a result, the victims may go uncompensated; or else the damage is shifted to the state and its institutions.

Legality as Despotic Governments Conceive It

It is a moral duty to comply with the law, assuming that the law "by and large" takes morality into account. Such, however, is not the case in countries that contravene human rights, for example. The duty to respect the law can therefore not be justified on the basis of duty as such. "Rather the legitimacy of the whole system of laws has to be attested. In this light the legal obligation is ultimately a moral obligation. It exists when recognition of 'the law as a whole' is a moral obligation," M. Kriele notes.[25]

The opposite of the legitimacy challenge posed by moral philosophy is the challenge from legal positivism, which Kriele sums up as arguing thus:

> "The law is binding, quite apart from whether or not it is ethically defensible. The duty to obey the law is a duty *sui generis*, based on the simple circumstance that the law has come about in accordance with the constitution or is recognized under the constitution as the law of the land. The ultimate fundamental juridical norm is this: the constitution in force must be complied with. Legitimacy then appears to be totally absorbed by legality. With this the binding force of the law is shifted to the binding force of the basic norm. In the end, however, this is not a legal problem but an ethical one...Only when the constitution is

25. M. Kriele, "Legitimität und Widerstand," in O. Höffe, G. Kadelbach and G. Plump (eds.), *Praktische Philosophie/Ethik*, Reader zum Funk-Kolleg, (Frankfurt a.M.: Fischer, 1981), 40.

recognized as legitimate can it legitimize the laws deriving from it. Whether the constitution itself is recognized as legitimate depends in turn on the morality of the systems of laws. The legitimacy of a democratic constitution rests on the fact that its institutions secure, on the whole, the concordance of law and morality."[26]

Obviously it would be impractical to expect of every company and of everyone working for it that they should vet each country's constitution for legitimacy before considering themselves obliged to abide by its laws. The fact that in Nazi Germany, for example, or in South Africa under the apartheid system it was altogether legal, yet could never have been legitimate, to discriminate against certain sections of the population may suffice to prove the relevance of that statement.

The principle of a global ethic underscores the relative role of the law as trustee of morality. In the experience of those who drafted the Declaration:

- a better world order cannot be created, let alone imposed, with laws, directives, and conventions alone;
- peace, justice, and preservation of the earth depend on the readiness of perceptive people to work to establish an efficacious regime of law;
- because an engagement on behalf of justice and freedom presupposes awareness of responsibility and obligations, people's minds and hearts must both be enlisted; and
- law without morality cannot long endure.[27]

Thus by observing market preferences and the laws, people can be encouraged up to a certain point to act lawfully and in consonance with the public interest. Yet that still falls short of securing the purposeful and deliberate translation of individual and institutional morality into practice. Market acceptance and adherence to the law provide no incentive to practicing "justice as a virtue," for example. This only comes to pass, Höffe notes,

> "when despite superior power and intelligence one does not seek to get the better of others or when someone—be it as legislator, judge, teacher, parent, fellow citizen [or industrialist, politician,

---

26. Ibid. 45 ff.
27. H. Küng and K.-J. Kuschel (eds.), *Erklärung zum Weltethos: Die Deklaration des Parlaments der Weltreligionen* (Munich, Zürich: Piper, 1993), 23 f.

merchant, employee, and so on—Authors]—lets himself or herself be guided in what he or she does by the idea of impartial justice, even though gaps and gray areas may exist in the law and morality or making law and morality prevail seems highly improbable."[28]

The fact that a company legally pursues the profit principle and is successful in the market does not of itself mean that whatever it does to achieve its goals is ethically blameless, nor of course that what it does is suspect. Given that within the law and the market there are elastic spaces open to varying ethical interpretations, a need for further ethical reflection exists. But what should it focus on: businesses as institutions, or the people who work for them?

10. Are Companies Moral Agents?

Morally considered, institutions are odd creatures. As Thomas Donaldson once put it, they have no butt to be kicked and no soul to be damned. They do not have a conscience that will not let them sleep or a body that can be thrown into prison. Hence the question: do business organizations possess a recognizable and influenceable identity by dint of which they qualify as moral agents? Or do they merely represent an aggregation of individuals who bear a direct, personal responsibility for their actions—actions for which the organization as such cannot be made accountable? As both viewpoints can be persuasively argued, there is no simple answer.

Companies As Moral Agents

There are a number of good reasons to assign business (and other) organizations the status of moral agents, one of them being the fact that companies are "legal entities." That is, their legal existence independent of their membership makes them bearers of rights and obligations. Hans Geser even sees organizations as having a greater moral capability than individuals in that companies, unlike natural persons, cannot exonerate themselves by pleading diminished *compos mentis* or other extenuating circumstances. "Only natural persons, never organized agencies, are allowed to portray themselves as the innocent victims of misdevelopment such as neglect in early childhood or subcultural pressures, or—having

---

28. O. Höffe (ed.), *Lexikon der Ethik*, op. cit., s.v. "Gerechtigkeit," 75.

recourse to 'human fallibility'—on occasion to act thoughtlessly, even heedlessly."[29]

On the basis of their ability to mobilize human and other resources in the service of goals and priorities, Geser finds it reasonable to attribute to organizations "an unlimited capacity for perfecting themselves" without making the Utopian "perfect human being" a necessary part of the process. The amassment of qualifications together with their cognitive, scientific, and technical prowess gives organizations "a far greater and steadier capacity for implementing complex courses of action…and it may reasonably be expected of them that they maintain those qualifications dependably and, over time, amplify them."[30]

A human body consists of a host of cells, yet the person who inhabits it embodies infinitely more than the sum of the cell's properties. The same applies to companies and their ranks. Organizations are better equipped than individuals to attend to various matters simultaneously— for example, while carrying on normal operations to concern themselves with constituting, modifying, and explicating the norms that should govern what they do. In this perspective, the establishment of every possible institutional underpinning conducive to "self-perfecting" defines an important aspect of corporate morality.

Whether or not a company can be regarded as a moral "collective" depends above all on how much freedom of action it grants its employees. Only in organizations where people are free to choose among a number of options can individual responsibility be exercised. If personal freedom of action is lacking, or so slight as to be negligible, then the chief focus of ethical scrutiny will not be the virtuousness of those who work for an organization but the structural rigidity of the organization and its leadership principles.

In connection with this point, some authors upbraid various institutions for inflicting "structural violence" on their members. Coined by the Norwegian peace researcher Johan Galtung, this term has been applied to the unjust feudal systems and inequitable power relationships, with all the inequalities they imply, that are, unfortunately, still typical in quite a number of developing countries.[31] In contrast to personal

---

29. H. Geser, "Organisationen als moralische Akteure: Ein Thesenpapier," *Arbeitshefte für ethische Forschung*, no. 21, (Zürich, April 1989): 30.

30. Ibid. 33 f.

31. See J. Galtung, "Gewalt, Frieden und Friedensforschung," in D. Senghaas (ed.), *Kritische Friedensforschung*, (Frankfurt a.M.: Suhrkamp, 1971), 55 ff.

violence, which can be laid at the door of the person who commits it, structural violence works anonymously.

Rupert Lay discerns this phenomenon—which, as he says, is inseparable from an appalling process of dehumanization—at work in companies, too.[32] In Lay's view it is not individuals who impede the full development of human potential, but systems and their "agents."[33] The French philosopher Michel Foucault pointed out that highly subtle "means of correct training" suffice to produce "docile bodies".[34] One of the most impressive depictions of how institutions condition people through their "trustees of power" has been given by Eugen Drewermann in *Clerics: Psychogram of an Ideal*.[35] Presumably the author did not have congruencies and similarities in the structural features of ecclesiastical institutions and their counterparts in the secular realm in mind, and yet they are obvious. Even today it is still possible, he writes, for someone who is active on the public speaking circuit

> "to fall into disfavor with his bishop because at some point or other in the course of a lecture a dear old acquaintance of that worthy has understood a dialectical argument undialectically or simply misinterpreted a 'for the sake of illustration' objection brought up by the speaker as expressing his own opinion. Forthwith this auditor, out of deepest concern for upholding the purity of Christian doctrine, feels called upon to communicate in writing his misgivings in regard to the teacher of 'heresy.' ...That is why just a few people who have access to the 'right' channels are still able to block long overdue changes in outlook. In almost every instance the process fomented by suspicion takes the suspicion to be grounded in fact, in fealty to the old adage: Where there's smoke, there's fire."[36]

In his analysis of the moral posture of business concerns, James Waters has identified seven "organizational barriers" that prevent the individual employee from initiating change.[37]

32. R. Lay, *Die Macht der Moral: Unternehmenserfolg durch ethisches Management* (Düsseldorf: Econ, 1993), 9.

33. See R. Lay, *Kommunikation für Manager* (Düsseldorf: Econ, 1989), 69.

34. M. Foucault, *Überwachen und Strafen: Die Geburt des Gefängnisses* (Frankfurt a.M.: Suhrkamp, 1976), 220-250.

35. E. Drewermann, *Kleriker: Psychogramm eines Ideals*, 8th ed. (Olten, Freiburg i.Br.: Walter, 1990).

36. Ibid. 241.

37. J. Waters, "Corporate Morality as an Organizational Phenomenon," in *Organizational Dynamics* (Spring 1978): 3-18.

Barrier 1: Strong role models. Like every social configuration, corporations are matrices of socialization where individuals learn to adapt to certain requirements that determine roles and ways of acting. In this process of adaptation, the individual personality and conscience may be largely surrendered to collective norms by internalizing and imitating the roles that "significant others" play. When this happens, there results "a fixation on authority through thick and thin, in a constant state of alertness to catch the pronouncement from on high, be it good or be it bad."[38] Where a person's own value judgments and moral convictions deviate from those of the surroundings, stress ensues. People then have to choose between conformity and resistance. More often than not they choose to conform.

Barrier 2: Strict chains of command. Rigid "official channels," with the authority they confer to issue orders, make it difficult for an employee to protest when ethical conflicts arise. It is particularly ticklish when a direct superior orders what the employee feels to be an immoral course of action. "No one may expect from a person in office that he should do more or other than his duty," Drewermann notes, "and it is a salient part of his duty not to disrupt or block the objectively designated chain of authority with his personal comments or intervention. An official in office has by definition to be the personification of the commonality and nothing else."[39] The recipient of an order "is thus not responsible for the content of the order but only for the form in which it is carried out"; in other words, "in his official capacity he may never break out of the prison in which his inner being is confined."[40]

Added to this are the steep information gradients and well-calibrated information filters separating the recipients of orders and their superiors, who relish being in the know so much that "subjectively they can arrogate to themselves the right to pin the label *Dummkopf* (idiot) on anyone who contradicts them; and they carry on as if they were the Truly Chosen— the whole show depends on them! However, what actually results from such splendiferousness is mostly far less splendid."[41]

Barrier 3: Group narcissism. People who work closely together every day develop a feeling of belonging together. Of itself this is a positive thing. But encouraging the solidarity and cohesion of the group also

38. Drewermann, *Kleriker*, op. cit., 242.
39. Ibid. 111.
40. Ibid. 112, 122.
41. Ibid. 166.

makes it easier to manipulate by appealing to egocentrical prejudices and glossing over inferiority complexes. Often inherent in group solidarity is a pronounced narcissistic element, quite probably the most dangerous consequences of which are a loss of the capacity for rational judgment and sequestration from other departments or work teams. Whatever the self-centered group views as being worthy of interest is therefore considered so not on the basis of objective criteria but rather of innerdirected groupthink. Whatever comes out of the group is automatically highly prized, its actual quality not decisive. Conversely, the "outside world" is looked on as inferior.

A feature virtually inherent in the group narcissism phenomenon is submission to a boss figure, and the greater his or her territory of power, the more superior to other groups or departments do that individual's followers feel. The aura of gravitas that the boss radiates is reflected back in the form of underlings' servility. This, of course, flatters the boss's sense of self-importance, which depends for its satisfaction on the narcissistic make-up of the group.

Best suited for membership in the clique are persons who are themselves exceptionally narcissistic, since without such types the energy involved in aggrandizing their self-esteem by running down others could scarcely be summoned. Every one of the band of "we happy few" is able to indulge personal narcissism; in the self-styled elite company, the individual ceases to be himself or herself: he or she turns into a ritual emulator of the personality model that the superior puts on parade. Preceding obedience by espousing an opinion that the superior may not even have expressly given voice to but merely hinted at outweighs the desire to think critically, to judge rationally, and to act in accordance with facts. "Reasonable" no longer has anything to do with reason; what "reasonable" signifies is "we are all agreed." And when the chorus vocalizes to the tune of "we really have to..." or "one really ought to..." (whom-ever "one" may be), the "we" feeling, as contrasted with the "I" feeling, can be wallowed in to the full. In the bosom of the group, pathological self-puffery becomes sanctified as loyalty.

It would be incorrect to suppose that the prime motivation behind this act of narcissistic symbiosis is the lure of a pay raise. The prospect of a higher salary bracket plays only a minor role at most in the whole sorry charade. No, from the standpoint of the personnel budget what makes fostering group narcissism so cost-effective is that bonuses of an altogether different sort suffice: the bonbon of a jovial greeting from the boss in the lift and his or her perfunctory inquiry about how things are with you; the prestige attached to an invitation to a business lunch or to a meeting; where the humiliation of being kept waiting in the boss's anteroom cannot dim the glow that comes from imagining how envious the others will be when they get to hear. Fanning intra-group rivalry to get into the good graces of the boss does not conflict with the group's extroverted competitive posture; rather, it serves as a selective mechanism for breeding subservient spirits.

Barrier 4: Ambivalent priorities. Because inconsistent or even mutually exclusive corporate objectives lack generally binding force, they leave the door wide open to arbitrarily fixed goals that depend entirely on random or personal interests and inclinations, and where the only thing that counts is whether the means to a given end work.

Barrier 5: Disjunctive spheres of responsibility. In large, tightly hierarchical organizations, quantified targets—relating to sales or cost-cutting, for example—can be laid down from "higher up," with the responsibility for choosing which means should be used to reach them left unspecified. The consequences can be problematic. "Subordinates" are simply expected to see to it that the targets are achieved—how that is done is up to them. They are left to cope all by themselves with any moral problems that may crop up.

Barrier 6: Strict division of labor. As in the case of strict chains of command, extreme vertically structured job specialization and division of work can lead to moral problems. The reason is that, while handling assignments requiring very special knowledge for their completion may in itself be ethically incontestable or inconsequential, when blended into the full kaleidoscope of interdepartmental operations it may turn out to contribute to an effect that is unethical.

Barrier 7: Protection against external intervention. This barrier goes up when a company blocks off any discussion of itself and its affairs outside its walls. In James Waters' opinion, and that of Eugen Drewermann as well, this can result in deferring needed internal reforms and prolonging ethically problematic situations.

Eventually all these organizational barriers inflict damage on the company—naturally, most grievously when they occur in combination. A critical examination of the reigning corporate culture and oganizational structure that erect or permit such barriers is therefore indispensable.

Corporate Culture

By this term we understand, analogously to culture as generally conceived, the totality of the value-orientations that are felt to be held in common and are adopted as self-evident in a company. These value orientations, most notably when they are credibly exemplified "at the top," shape the decisions, actions, and behavior of the people in the organization and are fundamental to determining their perception of what is significant, sensible, and seemly. They also codify the goals that the company should strive for and the manner in which they should be achieved. In the course of time, they become assimilated beyond question.

The corporate culture exerts a direct influence on the ethical "climate" in a company. For this reason, not only its employees' individual ethics but also its culture is relevant to critical evaluation of a company.[42] Bernd Oppenrieder considers corporate culture cogent enough to bring about value-loaded attitudes that only apply in the world of work and "are often diametrically opposed to the standards that apply in private life."[43] Corporate cultures manifest themselves in patterns of behavior peculiar to a company, in ceremonials and quirks of diction that provide the employee population with a kind of "cultural identity" that sets them apart from the world out there. And deviations from a culture's norms, though almost impossible to pin down or to describe other than obliquely, provoke negative sanctions.

Taking a company as a whole, the same mechanism prevails as that sketched above for group narcissism—as Rupert Lay puts it, a system of "closed-ranks morality."[44] Everything that comes from outside, from the world beyond company premises, is reacted to defensively. From employees, a hermetic corporate culture expects not independent, carefully considered actions but conforming behavior. An authoritarian style of leadership thus typifies it. Orders are to be followed, if need be under pressure; in this situation, people at the receiving end do not

---

42. On the issue of "ethical work climate," see B. Victor and J.B. Cullen, "The Organizational Base of Ethical Work Climates," in *Administrative Science Quarterly*, vol. 33 (March 1988): 101-125; G. Soutar, M.M. McNeil, and C. Molster, "The Impact of the Work Environment on Ethical Decision Making: Some Australian Evidence," in *Journal of Business Ethics*, vol. 13, no. 5 (1994): 327-339.

43. B. Oppenrieder, "Implementationsprobleme einer Unternehmensethik," in Lehrstuhl für allgemeine Betriebswirtschaftslehre und Unternehmensführung der Universität Erlangen-Nürnberg (ed.), *Diskussionsbeiträge*, no. 34 (1986), 38.

44. See R. Lay, *Die Macht der Moral: Unternehmenserfolg durch ethisches Management*, op. cit. 39 ff.

question whether the orders are ethical or not. As a result of experiments he carried out (see Chapter 18), Stanley Milgram concluded that a person feels responsible for his or her actions only if the individual senses that they spring from a "real self."[45]

An "open-minded morality," in contrast, takes its bearings not from the intramural reality of an institution but from the compatibility of human conduct with the general welfare. From the human beings who constitute the social system, this demands critical virtues: the courage to stand up for convictions, the ability to have conflicts openly, and a readiness to shoulder responsibility, together with the aptitude for weighing issues judiciously. A corporate culture that fosters an open-minded morality expects its constituency to be ethically responsible agents who if necessary will call into question the system's own norms. An openminded morality enables a company to communicate on a continuing basis with its social environment and in this way to engage constructively with more than just its own concerns. Building a corporate culture answering to this description and then living it credibly to give it sustainability is one of top management's most significant assignments.

Organizational Structure

For a company, or any other institution, to work and work together successfully it is essential to allocate tasks and responsibilities clearly and to order employee relationships transparently. This mesh of relationships in a company includes both nonhierarchical working ties and the formally specified channels of authority and competence. In modern companies, however, directives are not issued as military-style orders. Managers practice instead a leadership style that seeks with persuasive arguments and a positive human attitude to motivate employees to give their best.

In order to perform an assigned job, a person must have two things: the requisite expertise and latitude of action. Only when someone understands the consequences of his or her actions and has a certain discretionary leeway can ethical responsibility be demanded of that person. The person called on to make decisions responsibly must first be empowered to carry responsibility. From this it follows that keeping people in the know, besides being intrinsically commendable, also benefits the company: well-informed employees are in a better position to bring their experience, situation-related know-how, and abilities to bear in finding solutions to superordinate problems.

---

45. S. Milgram, *Das Milgram-Experiment: Zur Gehorsamsbereitschaft gegenüber Autorität* (Reinbek bei Hamburg: Rowohlt, 1974), 170.

Doling out information in bits and pieces can subvert the ethical integrity of a collective effort in more ways than one. It undercuts the individual's capacity to assess how the consequences of what he or she does will fit into the big picture, and it poses a hindrance to taking on direct responsibility as well. When people are unable to see a connection between what they have done and the overall result, they come more and more to feel that one person alone cannot make a difference anyway. When this happens, an important impetus is lost: the stimulus that makes people want to be ethically above board in the performance of their job.

Private ethics and organization ethics should not be played off against each other. Nevertheless, we can identify and describe the areas of tension between them. The more freedom a company's employees have to exercise personal responsibility in taking decisions, the more will corporate ethics be stamped by individual ethics. And the more fragmented the flow of operations and the more authoritarian the directing hand(s), the more problematic structural duress becomes. The inference is obvious: companies must foster the professional and personal development of their people, and afford them the maximum feasible degree of autonomy in achieving their set goals. The elbowroom thus opened up contributes to motivation and creativity, and to the ethical quality of what they do as well. All that flourishes best in an organization structured in keeping with the principle of subsidiarity. It is better equipped to adapt swiftly to a changing world—to developments both discontinuous and dynamic—to spot new problems, and to take up new ideas. The flatter the hierarchy, the more empowerment and autonomy that employees enjoy. And the more decentralized the decision-making network, the more auspicious is the ethical terrain at the individual level. Broadened authority and discretionary scope, a greater degree of independence, and pared-down rules and regulations all contribute to furthering the innovative and creative potential of everyone who works for the company.

Empowerment does not mean the absence of controls but simply other mechanisms of control—for example, with respect to how well fundamental institutional values and aspirations are being lived up to. These controls take place interactively and communicatively; they weed out uncertainties, provide support, and clear the way for freedom of action to be put to use for the mutual benefit of the company and its employees. This in turn reduces what we have called structural duress to the minimum while nurturing a corporate culture and organizational environment that reinforces and gives encouragement to people's moral convictions.

Creating a "morality-friendly" corporate culture and an organizational structure with a human face is not the job of the institution, however, but rather of every person who occupies a key position of responsibility in a company.

People As Moral Agents

A company never acts solely as an abstract legal and economic body but always through a multitude of people working at various levels of the company hierarchy. *Per se,* therefore, social systems such as corporations are limited holdings where morality is concerned: morality, or the lack of it, is brought into systems by people, their value orientations, and their style of conduct. To be sure, every kind of organization evolves an institutional life of its own. Yet this fact does not lessen individual responsibility, but rather the exact opposite.

In the context of development policy, Ulrich Menzel discusses the "agent-system nexus."[46] He makes the point that whenever "the system" is made responsible for everything, the agents—flesh-and-blood human beings, that is—disappear from the field of view, since the only possible conclusion is that the "system must be changed." The same train of thought applies here: the social agents in a company have the power to change or to determine the nature of the system. They only have to want to do so.

People at every level of a company are knowledgeable in their field, have career experience, and are socially proficient. It is therefore incumbent on them to assume responsibility—for themselves, for those affected by the decisions they make, and for the achievement of company objectives. They also have the duty to stand up for the moral convictions they hold. If, for whatever reason, they fail to do so, they take on a family resemblance to those "unreflecting administrators of the status quo" whose nastiest specimen was the subject of Hannah Arendt's report on the Eichmann trial in Jerusalem. Depicting "the banality of evil," she wrote: "Not demonic evil, not impotent hate, consuming envy or destructive avarice were what motivated the mass murderer—no, there simply were no deeper motives. Evil happened or was allowed to happen out of thoughtlessness, because of an egregious lack of independent thinking, out of dull compliance with the routines that regulated behavior in a demonic system."[47]

46. U. Menzel, *Das Ende der Dritten Welt und das Scheitern der großen Theorie* (Frankfurt a.M.: edition suhrkamp, 1992), 60 ff.
47. H. Arendt, *Eichmann in Jerusalem: Ein Bericht von der Banalität des Bösen,* 8th ed. (Munich: Serie Piper, 1992).

Of course, we are not suggesting that the persons who carry responsibility in a company should be compared to a Nazi mass murderer. But if a flagrant absence of reflection has been demonstrated even where the lives of millions were at stake, how much greater must the probability be of its happening in less momentous situations that demand decisions? In companies too, presumably, "bad" aftermaths are more a consequence of thoughtlessness, of the unquestioning acceptance of supposedly self-evident truths, of self-righteousness and stereotypes than of malicious or ruinous behavior. Yet conformity to perceived expectations from "higher up" with attendant eager-to-please obedience can also be assumed to motivate and guide the actions of uncritical "agents of the system"[48] —though there are various empirical studies that show that immoral conduct cannot be put down to the corporate culture or the expectations of superiors and colleagues but rather simply to the notorious opportunity that makes the thief.

So it is *people* who, no matter what their institutional station in life, must as moral agents be held accountable. Even though a notable element of heteronomy lies in every decision taken in an institution—an element emanating from the "conditions that prevail" as determined, for example, by the corporate philosophy or a boss's deportment— nonetheless the decision is and remains an individual moral act. In pluralistic societies there is no conceivable situation where the collective can be treated as the subject of action. Rather, the real subjects of actions are always individual persons.

There is very little evidence of unalloyed obedience to orders in the corporate world. Anyone who wants to exert a moral influence can do so and in so doing can elevate the ethical quality of group decisions. As a rule, it is quite possible for someone to put up resistance to morally unreasonable demands without having to suffer unbearable harassment as a result. Admittedly, sticking to your guns may sometimes have negative personal consequences. When an individual's sense of values repeatedly clashes with corporate values, self-respect gives the person concerned no choice except to leave the company—or, for that matter, any other institution, be it a political party, a church, or a trade union. Before resigning in protest, though, every avenue for exercising constructive resistance should be explored, not only to minimize the hurt to the dissenting party but also in the interest of the institution itself.

---

48. See R. Lay, *Kommunikation für Manager*, op. cit. 69 f.

Businesses, like society as a whole, represent in a manner of speaking a "lattice of standardized modes of behavior," according to Popitz, in which "certain uniform and regular ways of doing things are designated as fitting and binding."[49] Yet the obligation thus laid down is not defined with equal rigor for everyone by any means. In pluralistic societies and their institutions, offbeat behavior is not just possible but practically typecast in prefabricated models of how to play the "character": "The rough-cut, grumpy, ranting boss with a heart of gold beneath his gruff exterior; the uncouth businessman with his sentimental affectations; the elegant lady of a certain age who nonpluses with her hoydenish mannerisms."[50]

So much is clear: the answer to the question we started out with—Are companies or are the people who work in them moral agents?—must read "both/and," not "either/or."

11. The UN Global Compact

For many years, the desire has been expressed for initiatives to enhance the "state of global responsibility" by looking for and implementing global solutions based on ideas, values, and norms that are respected by all cultures and societies. Since there is not and cannot be any "special morality" for companies, the "Global Ethic" requirements for companies lie within that portfolio of globally binding, timeless, and intercultural values that Hans Küng and others drew attention to in their work on the Global Ethic.[51]

The UN Global Compact initiative takes up these values and applies them to corporate behavior—in doing so, it is not only continuing an honorable tradition, it is also in keeping with what a great majority of people all over the world consider to be appropriate. For Mahatma Gandhi, "commerce without morality" was one of the "seven social sins," and a recent survey of 20,000 people in 20 industrial countries showed

49. H. Popitz, "Der Begriff der sozialen Rolle als Element der soziologischen Theorie," 4th ed., *Recht und Staat*, no. 331/332 (Tübingen: J.C.B. Mohr/Paul Siebeck, 1975), 8.
50. Ibid. 15.
51. See the important work of Hans Küng and others, e.g. H. Küng, *Global Responsibility. In Search of a New World Ethics* (New York, 1991); K.J. Kuschel, *A Global Ethic. The Declaration of the Parliament of World's Religions* (London, 1993); H. Küng: *A Global Ethic for Global Politics and Economics* (New York, 1998); H. Küng and H. Schmidt (eds.), *A Global Ethic and Global Responsibilities. Two Declarations* (New York, 1999). See also the document "In Search of a Global Ethic" of the World Council of Churches, www.wcc-coe.org/wcc/assembly/or-01.html.

that people expect companies to provide healthy and fair conditions of employment, as well as no discrimination, and to protect the environment.[52] Today, the overwhelming majority of people in modern civil society consider that responsible, fair, sincere dealings with one another represent a social pattern of behavior worth striving for.

Secretary-General Kofi Annan first proposed the Global Compact in an address to the World Economic Forum in January 1999. Convinced that weaving universal values into the fabric of global markets and corporate practices would help advance broad social goals while securing open markets, he challenged world business leaders to help build the social and environmental pillars required to sustain the new global economy and make globalization work for all the world's people.[53] The proposed Compact has nine principles, drawn from the Universal Declaration of Human Rights, the International Labor Office's Fundamental Principles on Rights at Work, and the Rio Principles on Environment and Development. It asks companies to act on these principles in their own corporate domains.[54] While there were (and continue to be) worries that the UN Global Compact might be a first step toward international regulation of international enterprises, the overall reception of the Secretary-General's proposal was positive.

The continuing warm reception has several causes—one of the most important is that the Compact is an open process of engagement, with few formalities and no rigid bureaucratic structures. In a situation where markets have gone global and major players have to commit a lot of energy to addressing societal skepticism, it is the right thing to do and in the enlightened self-interest of corporations not only to avoid negative attention but also to develop best practices of corporate citizenship. Excellence in such endeavors could become a new sphere for leadership competition. But the risk of being exposed is also high, particularly due to the fact that the Global Compact covers the performance of business partners and outsourced businesses, allies that are sometimes difficult to control.

The Global Compact is no substitute for good governance in the host countries of these corporations. The three key aspects of good government that have not lost a bit of their importance are: the form of the political regime; the process by which authority is exercised in the management of a country's economic and social resources for

---

52. Environics, op. cit.
53. See www.unglobalcompact.org/un/gc/unweb.nsf;
    www.unglobalcompact.org/un/gc/unweb.nsf/content/LSE.htm.
54. See the nine principles of the global compact under www.unglobalcompact.org.

development; and—last but not least—the capacity of governments to design, formulate, and implement appropriate policies and to discharge functions. All efforts for human development are facilitated by best practices in the way in which governments and their regulatory authorities exercise power and care in their handling of state affairs and in managing the economic, social, and ecological resources entrusted to them. Abuse of power and tyranny by those in positions of political responsibility, corruption, misappropriation of wealth, inappropriate use of public funds, or other offenses all prevent development—and misconduct of this kind cannot be compensated for by the private sector's adherence to any UN Global Compact. While corporate misconduct cannot be excused by deficits in the state of governance of a country, good governance and responsible business policies can create the synergies to initiate a "virtuous circle" for human development.

In addition to promoting the aims of global corporate citizenship and social responsibility, the Global Compact offers another aspect of great significance: through its Learning Forum it contributes a value-based platform able to promote institutional (and inter-institutional) learning of all the relevant social players:

* governments, who define the principles on which the initiative is based;
* companies, whose actions it seeks to inform;
* labor, in whose hands the concrete process of global production takes place;
* civil society organizations, representing the wider community of stakeholders; and
* the United Nations, the world's only truly global political forum as an authoritative convener and facilitator.

Participating companies are asked to post on the Global Compact Web site at least once a year the concrete steps they have taken to implement their corporate responses to the nine principles. Theoretically, such reports could also draw attention to failures or share dilemmas that occur as a consequence of implementation efforts. While it would clearly be an abuse of the reputation of the UN Secretary-General and the United Nations to put a corporation's best PR stories on the Global Compact Web site, it remains to be seen whether many corporations will have the courage to go on record with failures. It would be of considerable interest to find out what works and what does not. The credible corporate worry is that advocacy groups would pick on failures to prove that the whole Global Compact exercise does not merit support.

For enlightened companies, presumably, the UN Global Compact is not making any unreasonable demands and should not—at least as regards the core content of the nine principles—present any insurmountable problems. So is this just a load of "motherhood and apple pie"? No, because a new corporate challenge lies not only in the scope of the Compact, which is extended to business partners, but also in the breadth and depth of interpretation by critical players in civil society regarding the various principles, such as the two human rights principles or the precautionary approach to environmental challenges.

On the other hand, the concerns of various critical NGOs and advocacy groups are understandable. They have gone on record with their worry about "bluewash"—that is, that transnational corporations with doubtful practices will mislead the public with regard to their true conduct and in addition benefit from the prestige of being part of a United Nations initiative. It would be unwise to deny that such a probability exists: the record shows that corporate misconduct does actually happen. Due to the fact that human beings are imperfect creatures, there will almost certainly be some misconduct somewhere in a corporation with global operations. Therefore it is likely that areas for improvement will be found—in many cases not due to bad will or conscious bad will but to negligence or incompetence.

Although this would seem counterintuitive, such misconduct in some cases is not only a deviation from the purist's judgment on legitimacy, it constitutes straightforward illegal acts. While there will therefore always be some black (or simply unintelligent or negligent) "sheep" in any human herd, sincere and successful corporations are unlikely to make misconduct part of their planned corporate strategy. In today's media and Internet world, corporate misconduct will not remain unknown or invisible for long. Corporations that have signed the Global Compact stick their neck out and will be under special scrutiny—which makes it a matter of corporate wisdom to act accordingly and not try to fool the world. As a matter of fact, many national and international corporations have been on record for years as organizations that strive for social and ecological excellence and not exclusively for economic performance. Reputable companies therefore are not starting from scratch if they sign on to the Global Compact.

What would be the answer of the president or CEO of a large corporation if and when asked by the UN Secretary-General to protect human rights, to offer fair and healthy employment conditions, and to protect the environment in their own corporate domains? There are not many companies whose president would shirk such responsibilities. But the general commitment is probably the easiest part of the Global Compact adventure for a company. The real challenge is to translate the top management's "signature" into an organizational commitment for concrete action and into the sustained motivation of employees that it is the "right thing to do"—and to make it part of the "corporate culture." As the UN Global Compact does not mean corporate philanthropy but addresses the political, social, and environmental quality of core business activities, it must be integrated into business operations and therefore become part and parcel of all employees' daily work processes.

Why should a company consider implementing a corporate process such as the Global Compact in directing its behavior—on top of law, regulation, self-interest, and convention? The worst conceivable result of higher than "normal" standards would be competitive harm because the special efforts and costs a company attaches to such additional considerations result in net disadvantages for it. There are a number of indications that the short-term financial benefit from superior conduct does not exactly burst into the limelight—it may even result temporarily in a measurable financial disadvantage. It would be dishonest to exclude these effects as an option for action on corporate ethics.

On the other hand, there are many empirical examples in which unethical corporate behavior has caused a great social outcry and intervention from the authorities, and presented no favorable options even in the short term. In these cases it is easy to show that misconduct can be a burden on a corporation and that higher standards can be seen as an asset. A second conceivable possibility is that financial disadvantages due to social and environmental investments over and above those required by national law could be compensated or balanced out by nonfinancial advantages such as the company's reputation. The problem here is that investments are easier to quantify than increased opportunities from an enhanced reputation. Yet the public's view of a company depends significantly on its perceived contribution to socially valued ends. Meeting customer requirements in the extended sense— that is, acting in a socially and environmentally responsible way and using energy and nonrenewable resources wisely—is an important block in the mosaic of commercial success.

This "business ethics" point of view is shared by Secretary-General Annan, who expects that UN Global Compact compliance will help:

- companies avoid legal challenges to their global activities;
- satisfy consumer concerns, avoid critical campaigns, limit their impact on the company if they occur, and protect the overall image of the company (or in the best of all cases, even improve it);
- promote the rule of law, since the application of Global Compact principles thoroughly, consistently, and impartially in a company's global operations can contribute to the development of legal systems in which contracts are enforced fairly, bribery and corruption are less prevalent, and all business entities have equal access to legal process and equal protection under the law;
- build community goodwill, since avoiding violations of the Global Compact principles will help maintain positive community relations and contribute to a more stable and productive business environment;
- improve supply chain management, since the Global Compact principles can serve as tools to help companies select business partners that are well managed and reliable and that operate ethically;
- enhance risk management, since predictability is essential to stable and productive business operations;
- increase productivity and retention of employees, since a fair treatment of people is not only of intrinsic value but also leads to increased productivity; and, last but not least,
- apply corporate values, which can strengthen the pride and satisfaction of employees and the faith of external stakeholders in company integrity.

In times when calls for more regulation are becoming louder, compliance with the Global Compact can also support entrepreneurs. Where deregulation and a free-market system devoid of social obligations would lead to liberal-type excesses—extreme demands placed on mobility, conditions of employment not governed by contract, paltry and irregular wages, meager social contributions, and a complete disregard for the environment—it would not be just humanist ideals that were trampled underfoot: nails would also be driven into the coffin of the market economy and the democratic system. Many members of management still complain about overregulation, arguing that the straitjacket of state regulation prevents entrepreneurial potential from being fully realized. A good deal of evidence suggests that such complaints are well founded, and that "less state" could indeed stimulate entrepreneurial activity. But here too a proviso is needed, since freedom always entails a moral obligation and can therefore only be claimed together with its correlate, responsibility.

In the interests of credibility, those who wish to avoid further overregulation of the economy and promote the revision of misguided legal developments must show themselves to be capable of ethically responsible conduct.

PART III

OPERATION ETHICS: A PRIMER FOR STARTERS

Chapter 12 returns to the topic of why a one-sided orientation toward shareholder value is no longer tenable for a company that seeks to be accepted by society at large. The broader a company's spectrum of activities, the broader must be its horizon with respect to its responsibilities and whom it regards as "customers." One way of buttressing its integrity is to issue corporate guidelines specifying the obligations the company is prepared to assume toward those customers.

Chapter 13 looks at what companies can do to join the fight against corruption. Faced with a corrupt bureaucracy, a company can choose to leave the country entirely, but that does little to improve the situation. There are many other options that can help nudge a government toward better governance.

Chapter 14 discusses what should be taken into consideration when formulating corporate guidelines and what makes them credible, along with incentive systems and employee evaluations. The recommendation to "Dare to Dialogue" set out in Chapter 15 is important both in drawing up guidelines that can command a consensus and in dealing with the public controversy that many a corporate decision may entail. Because dialoguing must not be twisted into an end in itself or misused as a means of sowing confusion, the chapter takes a closer look at what constitutes an effective dialogue and the personal attitude called for.

Corporate ethics cannot be translated into practice if a company fails to take its employees' moral qualms into account. When something weighs too heavily on their conscience, employees may have no other recourse than to go public. Chapter 17 delves into the possible consequences of a head-in-the-sand policy.

12. Doing Right by Stakeholders and Their Agendas

Among the thorniest ethical dilemmas are those that turn up in situations where one and the same management decision involves possible or actual advantages and disadvantages for one or the other party involved. While stakeholder analysis can help a company identify the overlaps, it is of no help in deciding how best to attune them. Repeating the mantra that all stakeholders are equally important is not only useless but makes it even harder to decide. In order to set ethically defensible priorities, it is therefore necessary to determine not just who will be affected by this or that corporate decision but in what way and how keenly as well. Analysis of all the consequences and their intensity and clarification of the various effects and ripples—intended and inadvertent, obvious and hidden— that follow legitimate corporate endeavors is extremely important. And in practice not simple at all. Even while the facts and data are still being put together, disagreement over where reality "really" lies often arises.

The evidence garnered by communication researcher Paul Watzlawick and a number of other authors indicates that humans are inclined to search for a pattern of orderliness in the welter of events.[1] Once a certain pattern has been described, selective perception acts to make the perspective thus established and the input that feeds it self-reinforcing. So it often happens that people cling to their version of reality, even at the price of having to twist facts: "My mind is made up, don't bother me with facts."

Watzlawick accordingly draws a distinction between reality of the first order and that of the second order. The first relates to physical verities— those aspects of reality grounded in a consensus of perception deriving essentially from the fact that they can be experimentally verified over and again. The secondary order rests solely on the attribution of a sense and value to things. This reality is stamped by present and past experience and people's level of knowledge, by their desires, dreams, and nightmares, all of which shape their ideas of "good" and "bad" and how they define sagacity and stupidity. In this dimension of reality, there is no point of arguing over what is *really* real.

For the constructivist school of thought, there is no absolute or objective reality, only "subjective," in part fully contradictory views of reality, naively assumed to correspond to "the 'real' thing." Many social

---

1. See P. Watzlawick, *Wie wirklich ist die Wirklichkeit?* (Munich: Piper, 1989); H.R. Maturana: *Erkennen: Die Organisation und Verkörperung von Wirklichkeit* (Braunschweig: Vieweg, 1985).

scientists and philosophers under the influence of constructivism thus take it as given that every person as a prejudiced being "constructs" his own subjective reality. Anyone who believes his or her view of reality to be the only correct one is bound to conclude that those who see it quite differently must be either wicked, stupid, or off their head.

And so it goes in discussions of business ethics as well: differing conceptions spring less from a clash of moral convictions than from diverse perceptions of reality. Laura Nash addresses the problem with a battery of questions, two of which are central: Have you defined the problem correctly? How would you define it if you stood on the other side of the fence?[2]

The Responsibility Principle

Against Ernst Bloch's "hope principle," Hans Jonas set his "responsibility principle"[3]: what is urgently needed is not so much a revision and revamping of society but rather the willingness to take concrete responsibility for the here and now and its consequences. Jonas was convinced that with modern technology a decisive change has come to pass:

> "Modern technology has begot ventures and feats so new in their scope and with such novel objects and consequences that traditional ethics is no longer able to accommodate them.... Certainly, the old lodestars of "brotherly" ethics—justice, compassion, uprightness, etc.—still hold good with unbroken immediacy for the up-close, everyday sphere of human interaction. But this sphere is increasingly overshadowed by a domain of collective action where doer, deed and upshot are no longer the same as there where people rub shoulders. And the power of this growing domain is so enormous as to force a new, hitherto undreamed of dimension of responsibility onto ethics."[4]

In the face of the unprecedented possibilities emanating from new technologies, Hans Jonas called for a new ethics—an ethics that would expand Kant's categorical imperative so as embrace reverence for future human life: "Act in such a way that the consequences of whatever you do

2. L.L. Nash, "Ethics without the Sermon," in *Harvard Business Review* (November, December 1981): 79-90.

3. E. Bloch, *Das Prinzip Hoffnung*, 2 volumes (Frankfurt a.M.: Suhrkamp, 1959); H. Jonas, *Das Prinzip Verantwortung* (Zürich: Buchclub Ex Libris, 1987).

4. Hans Jonas, op. cit. 26.

will be compatible with the permanence of genuinely human life on earth." Or put negatively: "Act in such a way that the consequences of whatever you do are not destructive for the future possibility of such life."

Don't Just Cogitate—Empathize

For us "normal" people, serious things that happen far away, concern others, or will prospectively transpire only sometime in the future weigh more lightly in the balance than the trifling occurrences that have a direct impact on us today. Hans Jonas calls on us to bring empathic feelings as well as facts and ratiocination into our deliberations on matters ethical. More than 200 years ago, Adam Smith asserted this need to activate fellow feeling:

> "Let us suppose that the great empire of China, with all its myriads of inhabitants, was suddenly swallowed up by an earthquake, and let us consider how a man of humanity in Europe, who had no sort of connection with that part of the world, would be affected upon receiving intelligence of this dreadful calamity."[5]

He would, Smith imagined, "make many melancholy reflections upon the precariousness of human life." Yet when all his "humane sentiments had been once fairly expressed,"

> "he would pursue his business or his pleasure, take his repose or his diversion, with the same ease and tranquillity as if no such accident had happened. The most frivolous disaster which could befall himself would occasion a more real disturbance. If he was to lose his little finger tomorrow, he would not sleep tonight; but, provided he never saw them, he will snore with the most profound security over the ruin of a hundred million of his brethren."[6]

Let this thought ascribed to the physicist Hans-Peter Dürr suffice to put the human capacity for empathy in a nutshell: Without a doubt we would hit our thumb more often when hammering were the pain felt only one year later.

---

5. Adam Smith, *The Theory of Moral Sentiments* (London: A. Millar, 1790). [Online] available from http://www.econlib.org/library/Smith/smMS1.html; accessed 3 April 2003; Internet. Quotation in Part III.I.46.
6. Ibid.

An essential criterion of any attempt to form a responsible judgment is how seriously something affects or will affect an individual or a group or how harmful it may be to nature. Aesthetic impoverishment such as that wrought on a riverscape by the building of a factory, for example, can certainly mean a diminished quality of life for the people who live there. The jobs that the factory brings and other gains may, however, compensate for what has been lost. But it can be trickier when unavoidable noise or smells reach nuisance levels, and much more so in case of dangerous emissions, for economic advantages cannot offset loss of health or human life. The end does not justify every means and its "side effects."

As a rule of thumb, the more serious and acute the impact of a company's activities on society and the environment, the more stringently must they be justified. Anything undertaken against the will of those affected needs extra-special justification every time; a company that evades this obligation falls morally short. A hallmark of freedom, after all, is not that somebody else but people themselves can decide on the value and rank they attach to their wishes and interests.

Steps to an Ethical Judgment

Oswald von Nell-Breuning has reminded us that "industry and commerce do not represent a supreme or ultimative value, properly understood not even a self-contained or intrinsic value, but only an expedient value."[7] When a conflict arises between self-interest and obligation to the general interest, a person should, says Nell-Breuning, opt for the requisite course of action that is morally least encumbered.[8] This conjoining of what is needful with what is humanly fair and just demands a great deal of those who have to make a final decision.

H.E. Tödt has proposed six methodical steps to reaching a "moral determination." We could try profiting from them in connection with business ethics:[9]

- *Perceiving the problem:* wherein consists the ethical problem? Is it actually one, or does the problem exist on an altogether different plane? Whichever, the problem has to be looked at full-round—that is, sub-problems should be integrated into a broader context, enabling their ethical significance to be discerned.

---

7.   See O. von Nell-Breuning, "Wirtschaftsethik," in H. Lenk and M. Maring (eds), *Wirtschaft und Ethik* (Stuttgart: Reclam, 1992), 34.
8.   Ibid. 39.
9.   See H.E. Tödt, *Perspektiven theologischer Ethik* (Munich: Chr. Kaiser Verlag, 1988), 30-42.

- *Analyzing the situation:* What are the relevant nexuses? Upon whom, as a result of the problem this specific situation presents, does a special obligation or responsibility fall?
- *Assessing the practical options:* How, in a world rife with uncertainties and contradictions, do short-term and seemingly self-evident technical and pragmatic solutions to problems pass ethical muster in a longer time-frame? What consequences and side effects will they have?
- *Probing norms, qualities, and perspectives:* Which norms and standards should be applied in settling on possible courses of action and in evaluating the most preferable solution? Which considerations should have priority in certain situations?
- *Verifying binding applicability:* Can other people in this situation, and under the same background conditions, really act in conformity with the proposed determination?
- *Coming to a decision:* What results once the five foregoing steps have been gone through and collated? What upshot is likely to follow from the perception and the conclusion drawn?

Announcing general and generalizing judgments without having been methodically prepared turns out most times biased or even outright prejudgments. Hardly any situation is so clear-cut as to preclude reasons for considering a different way of dealing with it. Impacts therefore need to be ranked on a qualitative scale of their ability to interact, so to speak.

In Case of Doubt, Which Interests and Whose Take Precedence?

From management's perspective, a company's various stakeholders are not equidistant. Thus when conflicts of interest arise or obligations collide, in most cases corporate goals weighted in favor of the shareholders and employees will enjoy priority. But what is the position as regards the ethical relevance of such preferential treatment?

An example: should an aircraft manufacturer sell "dual use" technology that can be used for both the public health sector (spraying against disease-transmitting insects) and warlike purposes to a country with a record of belligerence toward its own or its neighbor's minorities? What elements must management take into consideration in such cases and how should it weigh them? Does it make a difference to the decision if the company is doing well and does not need the order or if its continued existence, and with it hundreds of jobs, depends on the order? If the latter, how heavily should the welfare of the employees and their families as well as of the shareholders weigh in the balance? How can we calculate the probability that the political picture in the country in question may change in the direction of a more peaceable order? And, not least, will the company's decision be influenced by the fact that a competitor is only too willing to be of service if the order is turned down—that is, if the country will get the aircraft in any case?

Now suppose the company decides that the interests of the shareholders and employees count for more than uncertain assumptions about the peaceable disposition or otherwise of the country's present regime, and proceeds to carry out the order, with political conditions attached but unenforceable. Does this mean that it is acting immorally? Or what about the sale of chemicals that can be used for making essential drugs and misused for torturing political prisoners? What is the form when it comes to machine tools that can make parts for the production of basic goods, but also weapons components?

Since political assessments are rarely altogether objective, it is extremely difficult to give blanket advice in situations such as these. In any case, restraint should be exercised, of course, and the opinion of outside experts sought. In case of reasonable doubt about the peaceful intentions of the recipient government, then no sale should be made— but in a lot of cases, opinions on what constitutes reasonable doubt will differ greatly. From the ethical perspective, caution and—when in real doubt—a forgoing of the transaction are indicated.

The same applies to pharmaceuticals: if the track record of a product that has been on the market for many years unexpectedly turns up data showing hazards that were unknown when it was launched or during the early marketing phase, the manufacturer must take action, even if there is no official pressure to do so. Certainly the company must also inform the authorities and the professional public. Yet this still leaves open a number of questions that the company must come to terms with as an "ethical" drugmaker: How to proceed if the newly discovered adverse effects, though relatively rare, are very acute? How is the danger they pose to the few patients at risk to be weighed against the drug's positive effects for most patients on it? How can they define a defensible benefit/risk ratio if the benefit amounts merely to patient "well-being" but the risk can prove mortal? These are all open-ended questions to which doctors and their patients would quite probably give different answers than would, say, pharmaceutical industry critics.

The real life-dossier contains cautionary tales of times when manufacturers, knowing full well that a product was extremely hazardous, for purely commercial reasons kept it on the market nevertheless, with ruined health and the death of many people as the terrible result. But there are also positive examples where companies chose to withdraw or terminate suspect products simply out of a sense of responsibility and without any pressure whatsoever from the authorities or consumer organizations: Johnson & Johnson's exemplary product recall in the case of the poisoned Tylenol capsules, J.C. Penney's taking back of radio sets in the early 1960s, and Johnson Wax opting to get out of fluorocarbons in 1975.

Arriving at a judicious decision gets to be still more problematic when patient welfare is pegged to product price. Suppose, for example, that a new tuberculosis drug exhibits a benefit/risk ratio far superior to that of a product that has been available for many years. The price of the new drug is so high, however, that it is beyond the reach of poor people in developing countries. Should the manufacturer take the ethical aspect into account in calculating the price, or should it target only those who are able to afford the drug? Is it even permissible to set commercial considerations against the survival chances of people living in grinding poverty, or is the provision of vital medicines a responsibility that properly belongs to the state? Conventional analysis will respond by invoking the laws of the market. But this is not an adequate underpinning for the ethical deliberation needed. Although a company must in principle always be oriented toward the market, and even though many developing countries clearly fall short of meeting their populations' basic needs while spending lavishly on senseless armaments and prestige goods, a company's responsibility nonetheless extends further than simply paying heed to the purchasing power of the markets. It may be well and good to point out that a certain developing country is not basically short of resources but merely affixes the wrong priorities for allocating those in short supply. But this rebuke does not contribute to solving the problem.

Especially where monopoly situations exist—as when, for example, a company comes up with a cure for AIDS—the ethical point of view tells us that buying power alone should not wield power over life and death. Where the ethical imperative is espoused, there must follow a creative search for ways of providing for patients excluded from care because of their indigence or a government's careless improvidence.

Companies can seldom do this all by themselves. In such situations they may therefore do well to seek out broader alliances—that is, to make concessions on prices and to commit themselves financially to joint ventures with aid organizations and other agencies engaged in bilateral and multilateral cooperation for development. This kind of teamwork with humanitarian organizations could also serve to ensure that medicines get to where they should go locally and as a safeguard against profiteers re-exporting them under-the-counter.

Certainly there are many cases where it is relatively simple to make the morally right decision. But where commercial considerations conflict with human concerns, the name of the game is most often complexity.

Ethical Dilemmas and Compromises

Ethical dilemmas are predicaments that force decisions between two or more alternative courses of action, each of which is more or less fraught with guilt. Very tragic situations illustrative of this quandary abound— those that involve life-and-death situations and inevitable suffering and grief. A priest who was a soldier in World War II experienced one such situation:

In northern Italy toward the end of World War II, partisans attacked a detachment of German soldiers, killing one of their officers. The commanding officer gave the order to take 20 men in the nearest village into custody and to haul them before a firing squad. As they were being lined up for execution, one of the German soldiers, a devout practicing Christian, spoke out against the enormity of taking 20 lives in retaliation for one life, whereupon the commander made him this cynical offer: he would spare 19 of the men if the protesting soldier would personally execute one. The conscience-plagued soldier could not bring himself to do this, and so all the hostages were shot. More than 50 years afterwards, the man still suffers from that long-ago decision that, although it spared him direct personal guilt, meant that 20 innocent people were put to death, 19 of whom he might have saved by making himself guilty of the death of one.

While a situation as starkly tragic as this does not arise in the business world, there are other constricting ones entailing painful choices and outcomes. Take, for example, the redundancies that have to be declared in order to save a firm from bankruptcy or to return it to profitability, thus averting the loss of everyone's job. Or the animal tests in pharmaceutical research that inflict pain on lovable, defenseless creatures in the name of ultimate benefit to human beings.

Ethical dilemmas, then, are not situations that confront us with a choice between an ethically enjoined or a forbidden course of action, but rather those in which we are offered a choice between two or more evils.

Not doing anything or putting up with a problematic situation can also be a choice, though not an ethically admissible one because it sidesteps the real point at issue: having to decide on which is the lesser evil. Georges Enderle suggests four rules as an aid to clarification:[10]

- Decide from a nonpartisan vantagepoint.
- Set parameters for the targets' rights, and with these in view, decide in such a way as to respect as fully as possible the fundamental rights of those who are directly affected, not letting extrinsic considerations of utility impair their well-being.
- Decide in such a way that all the parties involved receive the fair treatment they feel entitled to.
- Decide in such a way that optimal use is made of the available resources by adhering to the three foregoing rules.

Solutions to ethical dilemmas often demand compromises. A lot of people feel vaguely uncomfortable with this because of the negative connotations attached to the word—as in an uneasy or a shoddy compromise. But qualms bring us no closer to a solution either. In his "ethical evaluation of compromise," Martin Honecker points to two problematic possibilities:

- "uncompromisingness on principle," to protect one-sided interests; and
- "compromising at all costs," likewise on principle, which—whether out of easygoingness or resignation—does not hesitate to sell moral values and standards short.[11]

In pluralistic societies, it is virtually impossible not to enter into compromises. So a few pointers to working toward "good" ones may not be out of place. It is important to affirm with all due care, for instance, a scale of values so as to be clear about which values rank highest. With a scale of priorities to go by, a lesser good can be waived for the sake of a greater one. Compromises done in this vein are unproblematic. Those that sacrifice higher values to a lower one, in contrast, are ethically not acceptable—and most emphatically so those compromises that, as Honecker phrases it, "surrender the unsurrenderable."[12] They cannot pass conscience-muster.

---

10. G. Enderle, *Handlungsorientierte Wirtschaftsethik. Grundlagen und Anwendungen* (Bern: Verlag Paul Haupt, 1993), 85ff.

11. M. Honecker, *Einführung in die theologische Ethik* (Berlin, New York: De Gruyter 1990), 241.

12. Ibid.

Limits of Corporate Responsibility

There is no final or definitive answer to the controversial question of where responsibility ceases. Incontrovertibly, people must take responsibility wherever they are able to "act on" something. This, however, is seldom the same as full empowerment, nor need it be. Those whose power to influence matters is only indirect, slight, and possibly unavailing also carry responsibility. It can be exercised in conferences, for example, through active, well-prepared, and well-informed participation in a team effort to reach a decision on this or that matter, and in like manner through actively "interfering" instead of passively acquiescing in decisions a person has not had a direct role in shaping. But just as a person cannot be responsible for everything and anything, so too are there limits to corporate responsibility.

A person can only be held responsible for that which, as far as a considered judgment could discern, was foreseeable. Here stringent rules apply, however. Given the accelerating knowledge explosion and ever more sophisticated means of communication and information, it is becoming harder and harder, especially for institutions with well-structured networks of authority and state-of-art communications technologies, plausibly to give "we didn't know" as an alibi.

In turn, every discharge of responsibility must measure up—that, ex *ante* it has to be ensured, and ex post accounted for, that fulfillment of a responsibility does not imply using means or acceding to consequences that contravene other clearly recognized obligations. Thus, for instance, ecological or social responsibility must not be shouldered at the price of jeopardizing a company's vital economical health, but conversely a company's endeavor to maximize profitability should not transgress the bounds of what is socially and ecologically tolerable.

Finally, the degree of responsibility taken on has to be within reason. Nobody can be obligated to submit to certain or quite probable death simply out of solidarity; but a slight risk to life and limb or health—as for example the possible complications of anesthesia the donor of bone marrow that can save someone's life runs—must no doubt be regarded as acceptable. In the corporate context, the counterpart of this line of reasoning would be that while, say, a pharmaceutical company may in cases of emergency or catastrophe be morally obliged to supply life-saving drugs without charge or assurance of repayment in order to prevent avoidable deaths or senseless suffering, it would be asking too much to expect that as a *general rule* the company should give away its drugs to anyone too poor to afford them.

Decisions Need to be Broadly Based

Differing premises, where values are concerned, influence not only the argument offered to buttress a decision but also definitions of risks, and consequently ethical evaluation of them, too. What seems morally unacceptable to one side may be deemed unobjectionable by another. Thus one and the same issue—tests on animals in medical-pharmaceutical research, for example—can trigger very divergent reactions in people, ranging from total indifference all the way to moral umbrage over the violation of animal rights so vehement as to incite militant protest, including breaking into animal test laboratories.

In the interest of avoiding constant exposure to such clashes, companies should take care to ground decisions that have social repercussions on the broadest consensus possible. Where the decision-generating process is complex, dissident voices should also be heard: everything must get a full airing, not only all the facts but every shade of opinion as well, no matter how unwelcome. Maverick objections, however inopportune they may be or contrary to the majority point of view, must be rationally refuted or bested in panel discussion, not peremptorily swept under the rug as being unworthy of consideration or ideologically unacceptable.

What comes out again and again when you peruse various "misdecisions" on record is a lack of competent, analytically gifted staff able to provide support to the toplevel decision-makers in the form of disinterested advice. Undiluted and undistorted information and analysis not beholden to the system are a must for business decisions of high ethical quality. And one final point: because there are particularly striking differences in how ethical questions are interpreted and the pluses and minuses of alternative courses of action evaluated in industrial and developing countries, it is wise to try for an intercultural "mix" in the membership of decision-making bodies.

13. Combating Corruption

Practically every theoretical discussion of corruption sees close ties between it and poor governance. People with uncontrolled power misuse their decision-making authority to corrupt ends. They are able to do this because it is impossible to see into how decisions are arrived at and because accountability is obfuscated. The same political strata are in a position to obstruct changes in the conditions that make it possible for them to line their pockets illicitly.

Although a company cannot justify corruption or other unethical behavior by pointing to the lack of sound governance, it would be naive to suppose that problems that can develop only in an ambiance of flawed governance could be solved by applying the maxims of corporate ethics. Where the state regulates economic activity excessively, where a surfeit of laws and enforcement agencies chokes every display of private initiative, and where officeholders willfully drag their heels and give everyone a hard time in order to foster a "market" for positive inducements—in such a thicket precious little can be achieved with moral appeals based on precepts valid in the corporate context.

So without improvements in governance, the problem of corruption is insolvable. The main shortcomings at issue are these:

- lack of a clear distinction between what is public and what is private;
- obscurities in how public finances are handled, paired with nonexistence of independent control agencies, thus hindering presentation of concrete proof;
- absence of reliable legal machinery for preventing arbitrary application of regulations and laws;
- weak public institutions and no free press;
- over-regulation in the shape of an unwarranted number of regulations, permit requirements, and laws; and
- murky decision-making procedures hinging on close personal connections plus capricious interventions by those who hold political power and their abuse of it for their own enrichment.

As a rule, the more inefficient the state and the more "powerful" its bureaucracy, the bigger the corruption problem. Under such circumstances a company has only this choice: either it falls into line or it withdraws from the country. Neither, however, help to change the status quo for the better. In order to curb corruption, the countries where it exists must be "motivated" by concerted international efforts to make changes in their political framework, notably:

- Dismantling of over-regulation: The overload of discretionary administrative rules and regulations provides officialdom at every level with the opportunity to exercise its authority not according to the dictates of objectively demonstrable requirements but rather in the specific interest of the (often low-paid) officeholder empowered to decide.

• Reform of the public service with a view to abolishing ponderous and nebulous ways of doing and deciding things: In their place, introduce precise and transparent statutory and administrative regulations, together with efficient chains of decision, mandatory accountability with no exceptions made, and irregular personnel rotations in particularly susceptible positions (but with due care taken not to impair competence). Finally, effective, speedy, and fairly implemented disciplinary and punitive measures against corrupt officials and employees are needed.

• Revised hiring and employment conditions in the civil service—for example, more competition for posts, better payment, and ombudsmen—plus cutting down on arbitrarily exercisable decision-making authority.

• Public invitation of tenders for government contracts and for all planning and procurement or public purchasing contracts above a certain amount: Documentation should be made obligatory; public and open evaluation of all bids and justification of the decision taken is needed. Because corruption can only thrive in the dark, greater transparency is essential to overcoming it. Black-listing businesses that have been found guilty of corruption and refusing to consider them for government contracts for a certain period can also be a useful tactic.

• Establishment or bettering of internal audits and controls by higher authority, applicable to both officialdom and the business sector.

• Creation of independent commissions along the Hong Kong model and protection of freedom of the press. Even in industrial countries, big cases of corruption have finally been brought to light only thanks to free and independent media.

All these measures serve to reduce the motivation and the opportunity to indulge in corrupt behavior. There could be disincentives as well—for example, a performance-oriented scheme whereby public servants would receive a share of the fees and levies they collect.

Over the last 35 years, Singapore has shown what can be accomplished in a political and institutional environment of good governance and incorruptible leadership. Comparable national initiatives elsewhere deserve every possible kind of international support. And the opposite pattern should be penalized, for example by cutting back on international development aid and cooperation.

Where shortcomings in governance are concerned, a reminder to industrial countries to get their act together is not out of place either. It is absurd to allow funds dispensed for corrupt purposes to be tax deductible as "useful contributions," leaving the state as was the case German Federal Republic—to foot about half of the bill. Were they no longer deductible, such outlays would appear much larger in the cost accounting and there would be an incentive to use them sparingly.

Likewise worthy of consideration are the proposals to sharpen the grounds for punishment and, where warranted (for example, in cases of corruption inducing illegal acts), to admit the testimony of persons turning state's evidence as well. Further legal possibilities include extending the limitation period, tightening the law on unfair competition, and clamping down on profits skimmed off from or wealth acquired through corruption. Finally, as is already done in the United States, persons who have committed corrupt acts abroad could be made liable to prosecution at home, as is now the practice in cases of sexual offenses against children—in short: applicability of the personality principle in place of the territorial principle.

If aboveboard competition is held to be a legal right worth protecting, more stringent measures such as these are fitting. It would be an advantage to reclassify corruption as an "official" not just a "petitionary" offense, because then anonymous leads would also have to be followed up—tips that now lead nowhere if the public prosecutor's office finds the grounds for suspicion to be too meager. In Berlin, the deployment of anti-corruption task forces that bring together experts from the ministries of justice, the tax evasion commission, the auditor-general's office, and others—allowing information from diverse sources to be pooled and integrated—has proved highly effective.

Isolated actions by individuals or institutions will bring no release; only a concerted effort can. If whole sectors, or at least the market leaders in a sector, were prepared to renounce corruption in any form as a marketing device, not only would each participating company be in a more secure position, the show of solidarity would also be a more effective means of working toward the envisaged goal.

A promising possibility along these lines is the formation of coalitions together with Transparency International. To this institution we owe the extremely interesting and pragmatic idea of establishing "islands of integrity," a concept deserving of collaborative attention. Experience shows that no significant process of social change comes about overnight but always goes forward step by small step. Proceeding from this insight, Transparency International enters into anti-corruption pacts with a limited number of partners (companies and project patrons) to take on clearly delimited projects and endeavors to see them through. The first results have been encouraging.[13]

Yet the long history of corruption and the fact that even making it a capital offense in some countries has not led to its elimination shows that stricter laws, stepped-up institutional controls, and improved political conditions do not of themselves suffice to provide solutions. Nor do moralistic outcries against corruption amount to more than quixotic protest. What is needed for a solution with teeth in it is a concerted effort on every front—including the business front.

To put it more clearly: in the end, companies and their managements are not going to be able to shirk from doing their bit in the fight against corruption. Wherever there is reason to suspect that passive bribery has infiltrated a company and employees are accepting commissions or other personal favors, an internal audit is usually called in to investigate, and the parties, if found guilty, are punished. To treat it as a mere peccadillo when employees engage in such behavior actively goes clearly against good sense and societal honesty.

True, during the last 30-odd years corruption has spread like a malignancy, so that in many countries today it is almost impossible to do business without greasing palms. It is also true that sometimes a virtual state of blackmail exists that must be acquiesced to in self-defense in order to stay in business. All this notwithstanding, it is ethically not acceptable simply to call attention to the problem, giving voice to disquiet while shifting the responsibility for doing something about it onto others. Armed with the moral principles of sound sense and probity, everyone has a valuable and fairly reliable instrument for taking the measure of corruption in a specific instance and for deciding what should be done about it. Using case histories as practice material, the logical application of those principles could be rehearsed.

Unless a person wants to look on passively while morals collapse, and be implicated by doing nothing, it is imperative to take an opposing stand. A suitable way to begin would be to protect from temptation employees whose work might bring them into the danger zone of active

---

13. See Transparency International (ed.), "Building a Global Coalition Against Corruption," *Transparency International Report* 1995 (Berlin: March 1995), 21 ff.

or passive corruption. Protection starts where the problem can and does arise, namely with human beings, in which connection the Working Group for Security in Industry and Commerce (Germany) has drawn up ten rules:[14]

- Set a good example. Avoid anything that could lead your employees to conclude that corrupt practices—even including active ones—might find favor or at least be tolerated in your company.
- Secure a written commitment from your employees to abide by guidelines (codes of conduct) forbidding active and passive corruption. (See also Chapter 14.) Make it clear to them that infractions will have actionable consequences.
- Let it be explicitly known whether and to what upper limits gifts, invitations, and other favors may be accepted.
- Require full disclosure from employees in key positions of their financial or other connections to suppliers and customers.
- Hold training courses for employees on the dangers of corruption and how to recognize them.
- Appoint a contact person in your company to whom employees can turn for binding advice on criminal law and the company's own prohibitions.
- Appoint one or more persons in your company to whom observations relating to corruption can be reported direct. Make it clear that this will have no negative consequences for the person reporting.
- To the extent feasible, institute the "four eyes principle" (the involvement of a second person in order to deal appropriately with a sensitive matter) and, insofar as necessary, job rotation. Demand detailed documentation on everything that goes on.
- Inform business partners of the regulations in force in your company. Ask them to establish corresponding safeguards.
- Reinforce internal controls by upgrading auditors' professional training and prestige and expanding the scope of their authority. In case of doubt, bring in outside examiners or experts. Report violations of the law to the police and see to it that legal proceedings are instituted.

Every positive social change has to be set in motion by someone somewhere. An expedient corporate policy gives every company, and the exercise of responsible judgment gives every individual, a free field of action unsullied by corruption. That means responding with a flat "no"

---

14. See J. Karkowsky, "Vor der Versuchung schützen," in *Wirtschaft im Südwesten, Zeitschrift der Industrie und Handelskammern Hochrhein-Bodensee*, no. 12 (December 1995): 5 ff.

when anything smacking of corruption is demanded and most emphatically not offering bribe-money even before being pressured. The morality of such a stance is beyond doubt: corruption is bad for the people involved, unwise for the company involved, and unfair to the society it affects.

Here as elsewhere, of course, there is no such thing as a free lunch. Rejecting corruption can prove costly, for if a company not only makes up its mind not to offer bribes under any circumstances but to absolutely forswear corruption as an access route to the market, no matter how persistently pressed from whatever quarter, it is certain to lose market share in some countries. In a global market this can be painful, and especially so if the countries in question are very affluent markets or very profitable niche markets, and if competitors are without scruples.

For the moment, all there is to offset the palpable operating loss is the satisfaction of having stuck to corporate standards, for the individual example can alter a corrupt climate only marginally at most. There is also the hope that in time word about the stand the company has taken will get around, giving it immunity to undue expectations and coercion. In the longer term there is the further hope that when a social "cleansing" comes to pass, people will remember those who refrained from joining in the merry "così fan tutte" revolving-door game. To its employees and its social environment the lesson will be clear: this company does not just talk about values—it lives up to them.

14. Corporate Guidelines, Incentive Systems, Employee Evaluations

Corporate principles or guidelines are aids to ethical orientation and behavior that a company issues on its own initiative without being legally compelled to but that are nevertheless binding on everyone who works for it. Their purpose is to help work toward and achieve the company's business, social, and ecological goals as harmoniously as possible. Notably for internationally engaged corporations that have to deal with diverse legal, social, and cultural environments, official guidelines can be extremely important:

• They help a company recognize and define its non-commercial responsibilities.

- By providing orientation in ethically ambiguous situations, they avert arbitrary and ad hoc decisions.
- As a counterforce to increasing government regulation, they are instrumental in preserving private industry's latitude of action.
- They reduce social transaction costs.

Clearly formulated guidelines can bring a company a good way forward on the long road leading to realization of its ethical goals. Nor need these be applied only to employees; they can also take in a firm's suppliers and other business associates. Many years ago, Levi Strauss & Co., for example, has not only taken a clear and definite stand on such sensitive issues as child and prisoner labor and treatment of minorities, but has also issued a code of conduct specifying the criteria by which the company selects its business partners.[15] Novartis has developed and is in the process of implementing a comprehensive guideline "package" to deal with fair labor standards, corruption, environmental obligations and Human Rights issues.

To be credible, corporate guidelines have to be more than ringing, attractively presented declarations of intent. To imbue them with maximum practical force, several criteria must be considered when formulating and implementing them. A corporate code should offer solutions to concrete problems, not just pay homage to vague desires. At the same time, it should not be an unwieldy statute book. Corporate guidelines should:

- Go beyond the letter of the law; otherwise they have scant point.
- Also go beyond the usual "done thing" in a particular branch of industry; otherwise—again—what's the point?
- Incorporate clear-cut principles; sloppy, fuzzy, or pseudo-profound and stilted verbiage harms more than it helps.
- Treat the areas of company operations that are most loaded with the stuff of controversy.
- Be forthright—that is, not promise what cannot be delivered.
- Be periodically reviewed to determine whether there have been changes in the information and knowledge on which they are based, and updated if there have been noteworthy changes.

Corporate guidelines stand to improve considerably if they can benefit from the input of competent circles inside and outside the company.

---

15. See also Council on Economic Priorities (ed.), "The Denim Revolution," Levi Strauss & Co. Adopts a Code of Conduct, *Research Report February* 1994 (New York, February 1994).

Since the guidelines ought to clarify a company's stand on extra-sensitive social issues, they need to represent a consensus. Agreement on the ethics of the conduct that a company pledges itself to observe can, however, only be forged and tested through dialogue with relevant groups in its public environment. As a McKinsey management consultant has pointed out, external circles give clearer and more critical feedback than internal departments do.[16] In this light, dialogues turn out to be one of the most important instruments of corporate policy. (See also Chapter 15.)

Corporate ethics cannot be decreed from on high. So far this has not worked even with the Ten Commandments, no matter that everyone assents to them in principle and that they were promulgated and recommended by the Highest Authority. This is not to say that "up there" plays no role: it is of the greatest importance that company higher-ups should not merely pay lip-service to guidelines but live up to their letter and spirit. Management conduct shapes employee conduct for both better and worse, and difficulties in putting corporate guidelines into practice can only be exacerbated if they are at odds with signals from above. When management extols social and ecological goals verbally but in reality regards the bottom line as the sole valid yardstick of performance, codes of conduct become irrelevant at best. In a worse case situation, a counterfeit certitude gets spread around, and the guidelines end up as an object of cynical or disparaging comment.

This leads to a few recommendations in the interest of the optimal implementation of corporate guidelines:

- A program of communication must be mounted to explain the code's key points and their importance in the everyday life of the company, while giving employees the opportunity to ask questions. Information campaigns limited to distributing explanatory leaflets via internal mail will not do the job.
- To make sure everyone in the company has got the message, written confirmation is advisable. It should be made crystal clear that violations of strictly binding rules will have personal consequences up to and including dismissal, regardless of whether an offense has positive or negative economic consequences for the company.
- Managers to whom the code applies must be held to account—that is, in their employee evaluations they should also rate people on the basis of their contributions to furthering the company's ethical goals.

16. K. Ohmae, *The Borderless World. Management Lessons in the New Logic of the Global Marketplace* (Osaka: Harper Business, 1990), 5.

- Ombudsmen, a "strictly in confidence" phone line, and other safeguards should ensure that an employee can get a hearing higher up on whatever may be troubling her or him if broaching it with a direct superior fails to bring the desired response.

The Downsides of Corporate Guidelines: The Prisoner's Dilemma

One of the most vulnerable points of corporate guidelines is that they only impose a practical obligation on the company issuing them and not on every company in the same line of business. If the branch as a whole behaves altogether differently—read "immorally"—the company that does act morally can encounter palpable competitive handicaps without any compensating overall solution of the problem it has sought to address. (This is why the UN Global Compact, discussed in Chapter 11, is so important.) Notwithstanding this difficulty, there is no justification for abdicating an ethical commitment to better knowledge, judgment, and moral convictions. It would be tactically more astute for a company to try and win its competitors over to the ethical approach as the right one to follow and then work to have any resultant changes for the better accepted as normal practice throughout the industry.

If this proves impossible despite a company's best efforts, then management must bear the responsibility of going it alone, a situation closely akin to the centerpiece and epitome of game theory, the "Prisoner's Dilemma." Its premise is that situations exhibiting the same basic structure are ubiquitous in our social relations:

> Chap A and Chap B have set up an import-export venture together. They use every dirty trick in the book to milk the EU customs and subsidies laws. For all their wiliness they come under suspicion and are taken into custody. Detained in separate cells, the pair are unable to confer and agree a common defense strategy. So as to get an appeal-proof verdict, the prosecuting attorney in the course of one-on-one interrogations offers to let each of the miscreants go scot-free if he testifies against the other. The one who does not cooperate will get the maximum punishment the law allows. If both confess they get five years imprisonment each; if neither does, only one year. In their solitary confinement A and B have three possible choices:

1. Out of solidarity, they both say nothing. This leaves them open to only one year in prison.
2. Both go for looking after Number One by confessing, with the result that they are found guilty but sentenced to only five years.
3. One of them, counting on his sidekick's solidarity, keeps his mouth shut; the other one cooperates with the prosecution. He goes unpunished, while his accomplice receives a ten-year sentence.

Now which would be the best choice open to them? At first glance the answer seems perfectly obvious: both persist in saying nothing and get off with a year in jail. But neither knows what is going on in the other's mind: whether his pal is really still his pal or is looking out for himself first of all. So keeping quiet would be too risky—ten years imprisonment—for both. No matter what the other chap may do, the most persuasive strategy therefore is to confess, with the chance of either beating the rap if the other one says nothing or of having to serve only five years if the other one confesses too.

What makes the situation paradoxical is this: clearly both would stand to gain the most if they stuck together and kept mum; but at the same time the most "rational" option is to get the best possible deal for oneself, regardless of what happens to the other guy. If we were to load the adjective "rational" with moral implications, so as to make the dilemma turn not on advantage but on adherence to the highest ideals, then both detainees would decide on a strategy of solidarity—though only on the presumption that moral standards, cooperativeness, or a sense of duty were in character for both A and B.

In a society, a competitive environment, or a group where moral norms have lost validity and force, mutual trust is simply no longer possible. The only thing someone can still depend on is the undependability of others. In the end, the Prisoner's Dilemma can be overcome only if a person is pretty certain about how fellow players can be expected to behave. Communication between the players—in our context, companies—can bring this about, but so too can straightforward behavior in the marketplace. Bringing the problem of the predicaments that companies have to cope with out into the open or cooperation between companies that experience them (by joining Transparency International's "islands of integrity," for example) might well be the most effective response. As a "classic" of game theory, the Prisoner's Dilemma stands on its own. Yet in one form or another it crops up in corporate life again and again—and in so doing presents the opportunity to finally break out of it.

The Codified Conscience: Not the Best of Bolsters

For people who hanker after stability and tidiness, corporate guidelines can feed the illusion that a book of rules confers immunity to problems. But this sense of security turns out to be misleading. Corporate guidelines are not a Miss Manners manual of proper conduct enabling the attentive reader to handle whatever borderline situations or ethical dilemmas he or she is confronted with now and forever. Arthur Rich reminds us that every time a fundamental question of ethics "takes on concrete form it turns out to be one to which there is no unequivocal, reconciliatory answer such as would suffice to put one's mind at rest."[17]

Guidelines would provide absolute certitude only if they could tell us exactly how we should act in every conceivable situation. No set of guidelines on earth, however, could possibly encompass all imaginable situations and the right political, social, economic, or ecological responses to them, while too dense a thicket of rules would inflict terminal paralysis on everybody. The one exception is cases where what a company defines as completely unacceptable is explicitly ruled out. Or as the German folk poet Wilhelm Busch put it, "The good—let all heed this refrain—is e'er the bad whence we abstain."

So company guidelines can only map out a passageway between wrong and right. At best they can function as a kind of compass, showing us how to get our bearings but not how to find the way, as Pieper notes:

> "If you try to use a compass as a means of getting to your destination you have misunderstood the instrument; you cannot simply read off your vantage point and the path you must follow. The compass does not tell you either datum direct; it always just points in one direction, namely north. Nevertheless it leads the traveller to journey's end—assuming he knows where he wants to go and thus also knows the direction in which, from where he stands, his goal is located. In other words, the compass does not specify the correct route directly but indicates how to ascertain it."[18]

---

17. A. Rich, *Wirtschaftsethik. Grundlagen in theologischer Perspektive*, 3rd ed., vol 1 (Gütersloh, 1987), 18.

18. A. Pieper, Ethik und Moral. Eine Einführung in die praktische Philosophie (Munich: C.H. Beck, 1985), 63f.

Every ethically tenable solution to a complex problem requires more than a book in which one can "look it up." Reading the Holy Book of one's religion is not enough to make a pious person of anyone either. What it comes down to is an individual's capacity to weigh a case and judge it soundly. Almost 200 years ago, the Swiss pedagogue Johann Heinrich Pestalozzi underlined the overriding importance of this personal dimension when he wrote that no form of government could amount to much if a country's citizenry did not amount to much. One can also relate the same thought to economic systems: they can function only as well as the people who are their operant agents. To which we may add: corporate guidelines, too, are only as good as the executives who put them into practice.

Comprehensive Incentive Systems and Employee Evaluation Criteria

Many companies conduct periodic employee evaluations as measures of performance. These give superiors and employees an important opportunity to talk over, calmly and informally, how the job is going. As a management instrument, they furnish the background and basis of promotions and pay raises. Company incentive schemes are likewise widespread; depending on how well an employee has achieved set targets, they too open the way to a higher salary bracket. Both instruments have an influence in motivating people to give their best, and they therefore carry a great deal of weight with employee and employer alike.

If more than lip service is to be paid to ethics in business, relevant signals have to be built into performance evaluation and incentive systems. Failing these, it would be naive or idealistic to suppose that ethical principles will be lived up to in practice: ordinarily people go the extra mile for those aspects of their performance by which they are measured and for which they are rewarded. Most management staff in multinational corporations are tested in the course of their careers for their ability to handle responsibility in a number of areas. Their income and their prospects of further advancement may thus hinge on whether they are able to deliver visible short-term results.

"Management by objectives" and other forms of running a company based solely on quantified objectives can mislead people into flirting with unmoral options in order to attain ambitious goals. One example is the temptation to sell a customer more than the company has the capacity to absorb, so as to achieve a high-flying sales target and thus improve the chances of an annual bonus or a better job in the next round of promotions. So long as employees are assessed on commercial results alone, in ethically ambivalent situations they may see themselves forced to act in favor of their own financial or career advantage and against the voice of conscience. Many people would seem to find themselves in this degrading situation.

In the absence of broadly conceived incentive and evaluation systems, it is tempting to give the short-term payoff precedence over the long-term necessity. When this happens, the investments on which a company's productivity and its social and ecological compatibility depend over the long haul get neglected, because in the short term they only mean costs and—shallowly regarded—a burden on the balance sheet. That is why, in addition to the usual evaluation and incentive criteria, qualitative elements should be brought in. Since it often is not possible to gauge the ethical quality of management performance directly and short-range in monetary terms, the creative energies in the company should be tapped to come up with additional variables that can influence behavior positively and open the way to more discriminating modes of assessment.

Once a company has decided to adopt qualitatively defined incentives, the means to the end and not just the end come in for scrutiny. The more consistently they are kept under review and adherence to them rewarded—or deviation from them penalized—the more effective incentives become. Human nature is such that it assumes immediate interests are more important than far-off obligations. The results that look fine for a short while lead to undesirable outcomes farther down the road. One way of putting an end to the fixation on illusory short-lived success could be, wherever suitable and feasible, to divide employee evaluations into short-medium and long-range components. A comparable procedure would apply to cost accounting the employee. If employees are measured merely on the basis of how much expenditure they save the company, there is a danger that costs will be trimmed where they ought not to be—for example, to the detriment of human health or an intact environment. And the harm may not be limited to the long-range consequences for people and the environment; at some future date, the company may get hurt financially too.

It is not easy to settle on criteria for appraising moral behavior in employee evaluations and rewarding it with some system of incentives. If, say, a sales manager fails to reach a target, the failure may be traced to ethical reservations but also to inefficiency or laziness. Doubtless there is a risk that inefficient or lazy people will take advantage of the system, while hard workers get dropped from the running. Still, with a bit of good will it should be possible to plug this hole. It would be well worth the effort, because when those whose road to success is paved with devious ways and means get promoted or otherwise rewarded, every endeavor to elevate the moral tone of business conduct can only come to naught. All the thought and attention given to mapping out the right ethical pathway and to elucidating the obligations it imposes will have little effect in the end, if you do not succeed in transforming the company innards in such a way that morally enjoined conduct pays from the egotistical viewpoint, too, because everyone acts in line with the new norms—in short, if you do not succeed in making sure that the good person is no longer losing out.

15. Dare to Dialogue

> *What concerns everybody, only everybody can resolve.*
> Friedrich Dürrenmatt
> *The Physicists*

In his seminal 1962 work *The Structural Transformation of the Public Sphere,* Habermas argued that the competitive pressures of a free market economy eventually require state intervention and regulation, which in turn produces increased competition and still more regulation. Finally the state becomes a major player in the economic arena and is faced with what he called a "legitimation crisis"—a set of normative contradictions—such as the conflict between serving special interests and advancing the common good. A vibrant public sphere is the only safeguard against such a crisis, Habermas insisted. Some form of public discourse about common affairs (dialogue that arises naturally among citizens, rather than the sort orchestrated by the state), as well as an arena in which it can happen, was therefore necessary, he said.

The call for dialogue became a core part of business ethics in the later part of the twentieth century, and it clearly continues as a commonly shared hope as we confront the problems of a new era. International conflicts that bear on local interests, increasing interdependence and renewed isolationism, calls for diversity and pluralism coupled with new forms of destruction and annihilation, are all situations in a complex world context for dialogue. Although many still tout the promise of the information age, the need for discussion and negotiation persists. The struggle of our time is to build the practices of working together. This is the hope of a dialogic theory of communication; its significance far exceeds the corporate context.

Using the word "dialogue," rather than simply "communication," involves specific normative claims. "Dialogue" has been useful in drawing together alternative and often more hopeful understandings and practices of communication. For our purposes, dialogue can be defined as coming to an understanding on claimed entitlements and respecting the moral principle that bids me to recognize the rights of others that will be impaired by what I do. Because dialogues are open-ended exercises, the course they take cannot be planned beforehand, and their outcomes and consequences are comprehensible only to a limited extent.

Dialogue does not do away with conflicts, of course, but in most cases it does help to resolve them constructively. Four prerequisites of dealing rationally with conflicts are of eminent importance in this connection:

- Conflicts must be looked upon as rightful and meaningful, for they can inaugurate or speed up significant social change.
- Intervention in conflicts must be limited to agreeing ground rules on the forms it should take.
- Conflicts must be organized and channeled, for example in political parties, trade unions, employers' associations, and other stakeholder groups.
- There must be agreement on the "rules of the game" governing how a conflict is resolved.

Yet even with these stipulations, dialogues remain an open-ended process.

Ever since Socrates it has been generally recognized that human beings are inclined to mistake their subjective certainties for objective truth. In this misapprehension Socrates saw the cause of all the bad that people inflict on each other. We derive our certainties from, among other things, our psychological and social needs, such as the need to preserve our self-respect, to belong, or to succeed, and from our interests, expectations, and disposition. Truth, in contrast, demands interpersonal parity, to the exclusion of error and deception. A true statement is true for every person capable of comprehending what it says and of attributing to it the same or very similar meanings as the person making the statement.

In a dialogue turning on a controversial topic, the participants bring at the outset only their divergent certainties. While this can be intellectually entertaining, until the stalemate is broken they cannot move toward tackling their problems together. In order to reach a consensus, both sides must be willing to join in learning together and in this way—perhaps—to arrive at a new, shared platform of certainty. The path to this point, already mapped out in antiquity, is still a useful route to follow today:

- First, find out what everyone can agree on.
- Then discuss the remaining areas of disagreement in a spirit of aiming to reconcile them.
- Ascertain the consensus reached at this point in the discussion.
- Next, identify the areas of disagreement still remaining. Most times these have to do with different priorities in considering pros and cons or differing expectations where decisions attended with uncertainty are concerned.
- Strive for a fair compromise.

By fair compromise we do not mean the arithmetical mean between two standpoints. If that could be reckoned schematically, the simple recipe for success would be to demand twice as much as what one actually hopes to get. No, a fair compromise consists in a reasonable joint framework of action elicited through forthright argumentation and based on the participants' elementary interest in coexisting in concord. And this is exactly what makes selecting the parties to a dialogue so problematic.

On the one hand, the full spectrum of opinion should be represented. On the other hand, in our experience there is little sense in including fundamentalist-minded advocates of particular interests. They seem to be so bent on ideologizing their own autostereotypes, and so preoccupied with the public splash this makes that they would feel themselves downright compromised by any kind of compromise. They thus labor under a compulsion never to yield ground, come what may. If someone has to stand up not just for his or her own interests but for those entrusted to the individual as well, the person may be commended for fighting for every inch gotten from an opponent. But interests someone is defending on others' behalf also need to be seen in a frame of reference of the common interest and given relative weight accordingly.

So-called issue-champions often seem not to be able to permit themselves the luxury of objectivity. They have molded themselves to the opinion profile that works for *their* public, such that the slightest compromise could mean a loss of face or lead to an identity crisis. So the role assignment that defines their persona itself takes on the function of a hypothesis corroborated by every act that does not confute it. Drewermann notes:

"It is not just because they would actually have to fear for their professional standing…but above all because their whole mind-set is centered on proving statements that antecede the mind-set itself…Ideological reasoning adopts a given thesis as the unquestionable truth. All it then does, applying the stratagems of contemporary thinking, is to seek reasons that demonstrate why the thesis must be true. In the ideological carousel that which wants proving is itself premised as the foundation of the reasons adduced."[19]

Rhetoric is turned on as a means of covering up the manifest lack of supporting evidence and the ideological straitjacket. What little, if any, consensus still remains frequently amounts, is no more than making sure there is no dissent and that what has been acquiesced in is duly homogenized so as to come up with what in political jargon goes by the name of a 'platform.' Because ideologists, being of a stentorian kidney, outshout those who argue more quietly but to the point in the quest for the best solutions, it is not easy to shut them out or up. Even so, when selecting the participants in a dialogue, knowledge of the issue should outweigh rhetorical brilliance, and a constructive attitude to the whole exercise should be part of the price of admission.

Essential Ingredients of Productive Dialogue

Tolerance and Waiving of Claims to Superiority
Tolerance is surely one of the most important character traits that those who would be included in a dialogue must exhibit. It differs fundamentally from disinterest, noncommitment, or a fixation on harmony. On the contrary, tolerance implies that someone holds firm convictions yet respects those of others. Aptitude for dialogue and steadfastness are not contradictory. All ethical endeavours and also tolerance, as the Honorable Nyanaponika once put it, begins with meticulousness of observation. Rigorousness of inquiry is not the same thing as a tearing-down attitude.

Tolerance is especially incumbent on those who, thanks to the sizeable financial and institutional resource at their disposal, wield greater clout. If the partners in a discussion are unevenly matched, there is a danger that consensus will owe more to constraint than to agreement. Not only is such pressure unfair: it also drives weaker parties into putting up resistance with all their might. If power corrupts and absolute power normally corrupts absolutely, then the same can be said of powerlessness.

---

19. E. Drewermann, op. cit. 115.

Soft-pedaling the definitiveness of a person's own moral views is also a part of what it means to be tolerant. It puts a particularly heavy strain on a dialogue when someone tries to compensate for a shaky grasp of the subject by standing on the grounds of moral superiority. It often happens that insufficient distinction is made between the facts of a case and ethical value judgments. But those who profess an ethical vision are precisely the ones who should give precedence to clarification of the facts over their value judgments. The ability to take the correct measure of the emphases and priorities that a question entails is a moral quality too.

Dominance-Free Communication

Of particular relevance is Habermas' conditions of practical discourse whereby every actor affected by the norm may enter discourse; each participant must be allowed an equal opportunity to be heard; anything may be questioned, challenged and defended; no one may use force or deception. Cognitive, normative and expressive claims can be challenged, but need to be defended appropriately in terms of truth, rightness, the validity which is to be negotiated; and sincerity as demonstrated in character narratives and self-reflection.

In a constraint-free dialogue, closure cannot be enforced unilaterally. Commitment to the process and the search for common ground is necessary, otherwise a strategic as opposed to discursive actor can hold up proceedings indefinitely. Strategic actors use fear, deceit, manipulation to influence others, and changes in position do not necessarily indicate a change of heart, whereas the discursive actor offers open, honest, justifications when challenged and learn from discourse.

A further part of dominance-free communication, naturally, is the timely imparting of information, ensuring that everyone is equally in the know. People who regard information as a power tool will not find it easy to accept this proposition. If they deign to cough up something, they do it as a gesture of "rewarding" at most. But this is just another manifestation of the same high-handedness that dismisses as ignoramuses everyone who, lacking their insider information, cannot but come to different conclusions.

Decisive for the level playing field kind of communication we are talking about, finally, is the truthfulness of what gets articulated or published. There are numerous reasons why a public crisis of confidence with regard to science and all who deal in its currency has come about.

A big problem today is that even within scientific circles there are at least two opposing opinions on every subject. Which of them is to be trusted? This, of course, the layperson can seldom decide. To point out that different realities exist is quite in order—we support this perspective. But to go on from there and assert that valid truths therefore do not exist either is simply wrong. As one indication of how effective this line of argument can be, the truthfulness of what gets said at public hearings is mostly not even questioned. Instead the audience sides with the opinion expressed by whoever looks more important or seems more likable or whose "reality" dovetails most closely with its own.

The fact that many "experts" believe themselves entitled, by virtue of their superior intellectual capacity, to put forth opinions on problems that lie outside their field does nothing to build trust either. The generous use of foreign words and borrowed jargon is supposed to wrap them in a mantle of all-knowingness. The swift kick administered the spectator doing his common everyday best to 'get it' is intended to show him that what he fails to understand nevertheless is so, and rightly so, and supplants what previously was to be understood or what is at present understood by the respective authority. Because less eloquently served up, the objections and arguments presented by the "nonexperts" are shrugged off as unprofessional or nebulous: in logical parlance, "insufficient reasons." Against too rash a resort to this "main proposition" of every form of rhetoric that assumes logic to itself, Blumenberg sounds a conclusive warning:

> "The principle of insufficient reason is not to be confused with a postulated repudiation of reasons, just as "opinion" denotes not an attitude without foundation but rather one based on diffuse and unsystematized grounds. Restraint should be exercised in alleging irrationality wherever endless aftermaths indeterminable in their extent must be obviated. In substantiation of life as it is lived the insufficient can be more rational than an insistence on "scientifically sound" procedure and is more rational than cloaking preformed decisions with scientific sounding rationalizations."[20]

To expect science to provide final proof as a condition of taking action would be to paralyze our very ability to act. Every act, not excluding an act rooted in scientific theory, is tainted with provisionality. But perhaps that is not our real problem as human beings, for no matter how narrow the margin of uncertainty in scientific pronouncements may become,

---

20. H. Blumenberg, op. cit. 125.

people will bet on it when theory appears inadmissible and unbearable in practice.

The lack of consent manifest in many a decision, then, is not necessarily due to the quality of the decision itself. It could also have something to do with a lack of ability to carry on dominance-free dialogue—with hostile attitudes and a "searchlight" perspective.

Relinquishing Animosities and "Searchlights"
We can observe time and again how people take up a hostile stance the moment their opinion encounters opposition. From that point on the mind is no longer open to impulses or ideas emanating from other directions; it only takes in the arguments that come from a "friendly" quarter and therefore jibe with its own set convictions.

To illustrate, let us imagine a discussion on the utility and risks of plant genetic engineering. If an older and conservatively dressed scientist representing the chemical industry proceeds to downplay fears of possible risks, using mathematically backed proof to demonstrate the infinitesimally small probability of something going wrong, then without doubt the presentation will convince part of the audience. If in rebuttal a freelance consultant in his or her late twenties wearing jeans, a sweater, and sandals expounds, without using an overhead projector or other technical aids, deeply felt misgivings in the face of humankind's unimpeded impact on our globally deteriorating environment and rage at being at the mercy of the chemical bosses with their fixation on profit, that person too can be sure of applause from one section of the audience.

In such a forum, it is not the facts that determine whether an argument is accepted or rejected but rather two mirror-image hypotheses:

- *The Presumed Friend Hypothesis,* which lets people place their trust in what they have direct knowledge of and are able to understand; and
- *The Presumed Enemy Hypothesis,* with the help of which everything that is unfamiliar or incomprehensible is seen as a potential enemy that must be foiled.

Who turns out to be a friend and who the enemy when it comes down to cases depends, of course, on personal experience and interests and on socially conditioned preconceptions. So truth does not present itself to us unvarnished and never did. It has to appear suitably attired; otherwise it will not find acceptance. In other words, 'truth' is something like a cultural prejudice. Every culture is grounded in the principle that the truth can be expressed most plausibly in certain symbolic forms—forms that another culture may view as trivial or inconsequential.

With his "searchlight" theory of science, Karl Popper drew attention to the fact that laypersons are not alone in being susceptible to prejudices. Every scientific description of facts is also selective and dependent on hypotheses:

> "The situation can best be described by comparison with a searchlight.... What the searchlight makes visible will depend on its position, upon our way of directing it, and upon its intensity, color, etc.; although it will, of course, also depend very largely upon the things illuminated by it. Similarly, a scientific description will depend largely upon our point of view, our interests, which as a rule are connected with the theory or hypothesis we wish to test; although it will also depend upon the facts described.... No theory is final, and every theory helps us to select and order facts."[21]

The Practical Limits to Dialogue

In practice, a dialogue cannot be prolonged until every last potentially or actually involved party is convinced. So it is necessary to agree on guidelines governing the technical aspects (such as beginning, end, breaks, but also sufficient familiarity with the subject) and the content (demarcation of what is to be discussed). And there must be rules defining what constitutes a majority. Less than absolute majorities have to suffice for a decision, otherwise action—in leading-edge technology sectors, for example—will be stymied. The right of the majority does not rest on the erroneous assumption that it is always right. Nor does it rest on the assumption that one group has a natural authority over the other just because it is more numerous. Rather it rests on the absence of something like a higher authorization.

Dialogues are not ends in themselves. Dialogue is not the main course, but the starter. Amiable palaver is not the crux. No, the object is to have out the conflicts in our society straightforwardly.

---

21. K. Popper, *Die offene Gesellschaft und ihre Feinde*, 6th ed., vol. 2 (Tübingen: Francke, 1980), 322.

If participants in a dialogue evince their distress at this or that state of affairs, social or ecological, and give throaty voice to their concern, then the distress and the concern must be followed by changes in behavior in order to rectify the situation that is the source of the concern. "In matters of great consequence it is enough to have wanted them": what is this lofty attitude but the vapid romanticism of someone who takes an intellectual interest, devoid of any genuine feeling of responsibility—an attitude that Max Weber pilloried 80 years ago.[22] Dialogues lacking in what Jürgen Habermas once termed "precommunicative intention to act" readily degenerate into alibi exercises for Machiavellians who have not the slightest desire to see people change their behaviour.[23] For them, a dialogue is merely a delaying tactic, a way of gaining time. Yet nonaction may have graver negative consequences than a less-than-perfect course of action, as can be demonstrated quite clearly in the context of sustainable development.

In the ideal case, dialogues can even out interests or bring about a consensus. Admittedly, it is difficult to devise the conditions conducive to this result. The "job descriptions" in the literature detailing the requirements of dialogue leaders are rather at variance with real-life human beings. Complete lack of bias plus other-directed empathy would be among the sought-after qualifications, but they rarely show up in dialoguing as actually practiced. Or then the people actually responsible for whatever is the target of criticism are unavailable to take part in the discussion. In lieu of the doers, "spokespersons" are delegated who are woefully unversed in the material and in the worst case must serve as ideological mouthpieces. In any event they lack the influence that would ensure that what has been agreed in dialogue will be implemented in their company.

There are also cases where interest groups feel unable to accept the results that their representatives have brought back from a discussion— not because there was a lack of clarity on the necessity of joining forces to act but because what was agreed did not match their stated institutional standpoint verbatim. As the word "standpoint" implies, the slightest flexibility of thinking or any constructive effort or move to meet the other side halfway would have to be construed as a contradiction in terms. So we would suggest that the executives who have the final responsibility should take part personally in the dialogue. The trouble is, they often have other, more pressing business or consider themselves too

---

22. M. Weber, "Politik als Beruf," in M. Weber, *Gesammelte Politische Schriften*, 5th ed. (Tübingen: J.C.B. Mohr/UTB, 1988), 546.

23. J. Habermas, *Theorie des kommunikativen Handelns*, vol. 1, "Handlungsrationalität und gesellschaftliche Rationalisierung" (Frankfurt a.M.: Suhrkamp, 1981), 378.

important to "bother" with those who see things differently from themselves. A laudable exception worth mentioning is the church-business forum in Switzerland for which, among other influential individuals, bishops, Board Chairs and CEOs make themselves available.

16. Criticism From Within

Human history began with an act of disobedience,
it may well end with an act of obedience.
Ernst Bloch

"Sometimes one has to attack something in order to save it; sometimes one has to destroy something in order to liberate it; sometimes there's no way to avoid inflicting hurt in order to heal." These words are the rallying cry of Eugen Drewermann in his work *Clerics*, whose efforts to renew the Catholic Church have been met with hard sanctions.[24] He shares this fate not only with former colleagues and other likewise renowned, likewise failed "revolutionaries," but also with "mute unsung" heroes such as the autobiographical protagonist of the novel *Noli me tangere* who pays with his life—just as did the author, José Rizal.[25]

All these non-mainstream thinkers have touched the untouchable: they have exposed moralisms in order to impart new force to morality; they have rejected imposed obligations out of a belief in unconditional obligations; they have broken the spell of handed-down illusions in order to quicken awareness of authentic values. They have not sought to replace old values with new ones; they only seek to redeem the old values on different premises.

As the embodiment of habitual ways of doing things, organizations risk losing their legitimacy if they restrict their own people's critical perception of norms and their right to follow the dictates of their conscience. Because critical perception is inconvenient, tending as it does to try and change a state of affairs that has long been accepted as self-evident, it is frequently dismissed out of hand as "intolerable." And yet nothing exerts a greater conservative force than the capacity to adapt and change, and this holds just as true for business institutions as it does for church institutions. People who commit themselves to bringing about changes in their institutions out of ethical conviction or who speak out against indefensible shortcomings need all the fortitude they can muster.

24. Drewermann, op. cit.
25. J. Rizal, *Noli me tangere* (Frankfurt a.m.: Insel Verlag, 1987).

In this chapter we present examples of how companies deal with criticism that comes "from within" in two senses of the word: from employees within the company but also between employees themselves. Companies should look at such criticism as an opportunity, not a threat, treating it as preferable to criticism from without, for that which is today spoken in darkness shall tomorrow "be proclaimed upon the housetops" (Matthew 10, 27). Furthermore, they should recognize the innermost intention of employees who express themselves critically for what it is: a courageous decision to think, say, and do what their feelings and experiences tell them they must.

The act of piping up from the ranks to bring something dubious previously kept covert out into the open is called whistleblowing. It is fairly easy to distinguish genuine whistleblowers from the various also ran organization types: neurotic know-it-alls, niggling pedants, professional smear artists, revenge crazed malcontents, windbags, snitches, Frustrated Freds (or Frannys), and Envious Ernies (or Emmas). They are not in the habit of lifting a finger themselves; they leave that to others. The latter touch their forelock to everything that comes from above and goad from below. They project their own discontent into others and calmly take their distance while their manipulable colleagues fight their battles for them. They pervert their surroundings into an arena of their own neurotic symptoms. Should such people actually once stand up and blow the whistle, it mostly amounts to nothing more than a verbal demonstration at a point where the object of the supposed warning has already decided anyway to refrain from doing whatever he or she is being warned against doing.

For other individuals—those who have something to bring up that sincerely troubles them with no thought of personal gain—some kind of protected minority shelter is needed. We are all for establishing an ombudsman's office or its equivalent to deal with internal criticism correctly and to settle rather than shunt aside ethical problems. Because intra-company criticism as manifested in whistleblowing can occur at various levels, it can also have very different effects on the company and the people involved.

Levels of Whistleblowing

At the Same Hierarchical Level
A concrete example will best serve to illustrate this level of whistle blowing. Let us suppose you happen to catch a colleague with whom you

were on a business trip putting in for travel outlays that you know for certain were not as high as claimed. You have observed this big-spender a number of times, and every time precisely when it was at company expense. So what do you do—look the other way or butt in?

It is hard to pinpoint exactly where the "pain threshold" of a certain act lies and when intervention becomes unavoidable. Must the private use of company ballpoint pens be considered a no-no, or do we draw the line at pocket calculators or, upping it, personal computers? Are brief private phone calls on company time still within bounds but long-distance calls at company expense due cause for whistleblowing? Is it permissible to use company photocopying machines to run off copies for private purposes, or does a problem arise only when the practice becomes habitual or people overdo it?

It is possible to mull endlessly over innumerable such possible cases. But in every case the consequence for the firm is clear: even small, seemingly negligible "liberties" taken with company property add up to immense sums if they become common practice. So the short answer always is that company property may not be misused for private purposes, and it must be enforced throughout. But when it comes to whistleblowing or any other form of intervention among colleagues, it is important first to make sure the intervention is warranted by the gravity of the misdeed.

Where an offending practice is more than a fellow employee can tolerate, he or she faces the choice of keeping the misgivings quiet and going on as before or of confronting the errant colleague point-blank. Ethically, the second response would be the right and necessary one, since to gloss over incorrect or even illicit behavior is tantamount to colluding with it, to the detriment of the company, meaning employees and shareholders as well.

A direct and unsparing confrontation, while likely to put a strain on the personal relationship, might nevertheless help to clear up the problem. If it proves fruitless or fails to bring the desired result, what then: turn to the next higher level of the hierarchy? Doing so is bound to aggravate the situation, since the offending person may then have to reckon with unpleasant disciplinary measures or even harsher penalties.

Everyone's interest in working together efficiently and smoothly as well as common sense tells us that problems should be sorted out at the level where they arise. So blowing the whistle to superiors is not something to be taken lightly, and certainly not before having weighed the seriousness of a person's misconduct against the consequences that may be expected. Without this pause for reflection, a whistleblower opens himself or herself to being branded an informer or a self-important busybody. By way of a kind of self-examination of potential whistle-blowers, J. Vernon Jensen has proposed a number of questions touching on personal motivation, ethics, and integrity, along with others relating to the care taken in procuring information and in exploring other, more subtle ways of remedying a situation.[26] The object of the exercise is to make sure that self-righteousness and projection are not what really motivate the whistleblower.

At the Higher Level

Another hypothetical case: let us suppose that in order to meet a sales department's budget target for the year, important documents are doctored, reports are backdated or predated, accounts fiddled, goods sold beyond their expiry date, and so on. Let us further suppose that the likelihood of these goings-on being discovered is remote—because they happen in a subsidiary in a developing country, for example. What we have here is misfeasance that violates not only the law but also the company's own rules and regulations.

In such a case there can be no doubt that from both an ethical viewpoint and that of the company's own best interests, intervention and contravention are urgently called for. Since intervention at the same hierarchical level would probably avail little, the next higher one has to be called in—and this regardless of whatever ill feelings it may cause among the culpable colleagues, who quite likely must reckon with sanctions. The company interest is superordinate to individual loyalties.

In any normal business, the ailment would have been dealt with at this point at the latest. The following hypothetical "escalations" are therefore rather improbable, yet still possible. The state of play now is that bringing the responsible superiors into the picture has failed to set matters right, and all other efforts undertaken inside the company have likewise come to naught. So, because they are lucrative, the improper and illicit practices have continued. This being the case, it is futile to go on trying to pursue the matter through the designated company channels. The next thing that must be considered is whether to go outside.

---

26. J.V. Jensen, "Ethical Tension Points in Whistleblowing," in *Journal of Business Ethics*, vol. 6, no. 4 (1987): 322ff.

Before this step is taken, it is more than ever imperative to weigh the pros and cons very carefully. If taken, it could entail—in addition to serious harm to the company's reputation and claims for damages—great personal risks for the whistleblower. All the same, ethical and material values or commandments and prohibitions cannot be played off against each other to the end of transmuting bad into good.

Going Outside the Pale
There is a raft of cases documenting how company employees, acting on professed or genuine dictates of conscience, brought problems they got nowhere with internally to the attention of either the authorities, well-known critics of business, or the media. One of the best known is Dan Gellert, a Lockheed employee who went public with the alarming charge that the L-1011 aircraft did not meet U.S. safety regulations.[27] Another was Frank Camps, who alerted the public to engineering defects in the Ford Pinto.[28] Anyone who cares to do so can find further examples from other branches of industry.

While whistleblowers may be hailed as public heroes in cases such as these, in their companies they are mostly looked on as turncoats or overweening cowards who, in their craving for admiration or from some other base motive, did not seize every internal possibility of remedying a problem. The image we get of these people will likely always reflect the feelings that their partisans and foes have about them.

The risks that a whistleblower incurs in going public can be considerable. The literature is replete with case histories in which the whistle-blower, not the person responsible for the problem, was fired. Real-life stories by no means always have the happy end that concludes Arthur Hailey's novel *Strong Medicine* (1984), where the man who resigns from the company out of protest against its immoral practices is reinstated and promoted with all flags flying. But the opposite pole, as in the docufilm *Silkwood*, where the heroine who is out to blow the lid on slipshod safety precautions in a nuclear power plant is murdered, stands at the extreme end of the statistical curve too.

Whistleblowing has always aroused controversy. In a public debate in the early 1970s, Ralph Nader, American lawyer and critic of corporate behavior, pointed out that employees are the first to know if a company

---

27. D. Gellert, "Insisting on Safety in the Skies," in A.F. Westin (ed.), *WhistleBlowing!: Loyalty and Dissent in the Corporation* (New York: McGraw-Hill, 1981), 17-30.
28. F. Camps, "Warning an Auto Company About an Unsafe Design," in Westin (ed.), op. cit. 119-129.

markets faulty and dangerous products, pollutes the environment, connives with competitors, or covers up unwelcome data—on side effects of drugs, for example.[29] Even back then, Nader was addressing the questions that all potential whistleblowers have to answer before they decide to go public. These concern notably the accuracy and completeness of the information in their hands, possible breaches of ethics in acting or failing to act, and the pluses and minuses of taking the external versus the internal route.

Whistleblowing continues to be regarded as a last line of defense, to be resorted to only when no other recourse is left or only after institutional heat has been turned on the unruly employee. Nader demands in the public interest the right of employees to go public if they have tapped every last accessible channel of communication in the company without getting action on the problem they have raised.

Naturally, whistleblowers are mortal beings with strengths and weaknesses, just like everyone else. Not all of them have high and noble motives such as a desire to protect people or the environment, nor is every situation they blow the whistle on as dire as they maintain. And it is certainly not always necessary to become a martyr who, seeing no other choice, sacrifices personal happiness on the altar of last resort. That is why both the institution under fire and the alerted public, inclusive of the media, should always probe the credibility of the whistleblower's motivation and the correctness of the information disclosed. A careful inquiry into the facts could prevent needless panic mongering on the part of troublemakers who, because of some personal grudge or because their own unrealistic career expectations have been disappointed, spread horror tales designed to ensure that they will exit the company with a bang.

The immaterial and financial damage caused an accused business by superficial and sensational coverage in the mass media can be enormous. Against the public's suspicion that there must be something in the story—especially when the allegations, though not provable, cannot be refuted—and the media's cutthroat scramble to raise their circulation and viewer ratings, a besieged company really has no counter-offensive weapon other than preemptive, one-step-ahead information and communication. Efforts to control or repair the damage, however, are always more uphill and less effective than the blast of scandal, even when a company is able to prove its innocence.

---

29. R. Nader, "An Anatomy of Whistle Blowing," in R. Nader, P.J. Petkas, and K. Blackwell (eds.), *Whistle-Blowing: The Report of a Conference on Professional Responsibility* (New York: Grossman Publishers, 1972), 4f.

Broadcasting criticism outside the gates is always more fraught than mooting it inside. So to underline the point again: whoever professes to be motivated by loyalty to the company and to the matter at issue should first try everything possible to resolve a problem internally. The overriding motive of every whistleblower must be to put an end to a problematic situation, not to inflict harm on the person or persons who have caused it or the company, even when disgrace is the worst they stand to suffer.

Cases involving a danger to the public welfare or safety are relatively few and far between in any case. Most problems, however unacceptable or unpalatable they may be, are played out at the departmental or personal level, and these damage primarily the company and the people who work for it. The well-intentioned person who needs and seeks internal support in dealing with them will find it. We believe that most companies have trustworthy people in influential positions who are prepared to take such problems seriously and to put them right without making unnecessary waves.

Unfortunately, we also have a number of well-documented cases where employees, acting with the best of intentions and to the best of their knowledge and belief, tried in a constructive way to put a stop to malpractices or even unlawful doings in their companies but found management deaf to their suggestions or, yes, were "zapped" for their pains in the "kill the messenger who brings bad news" style of yore. Some among them came across flagrant wrongs and did their utmost to have them rectified internally in the interest of the company and a sensible solution, yet came to grief with very tragic consequences to themselves. This happened especially when, at the end of their rope, they turned to outsiders for help. Instead of acting promptly to save human health and lives, not to mention enormous company assets, top management played the offended party, stigmatized the would-be reformers as schemers and betrayers, and ordered them fired.

In every one of these cases the whistleblowers were later proved right—in some instances, by tragic accidents with great loss of human life. Among the best known are the Challenger space shuttle disaster, which could have been prevented, and the mishaps that occurred in connection with the Ford Pinto and with Firestone 500 tires.[30] Without

---

30. See the case studys by R.P. Boisjoly, E.F. Curtis, and E. Mellicanm, "Roger Boisjoly and the Challenger Disaster: The Ethical Dimension," in *Journal of Business Ethics*, vol. 8, no. 4 (1989): 217-230; P.H. Werhane, "Engineers and Management: The Challenge of the Challenger Incident," in *Journal of Business Ethics*, vol. 10, no. 8 (1991): 605-616; "Managing Product Safety: The Ford Pinto," in *Ethics in Management* (Boston, Mass.: Harvard Business School 1984): 111-119; see also Westin (ed.), op. cit. 10f.

exception the (ir)responsible manufacturers as a result shouldered a big financial burden.

Even when things do not happen that dramatically, the whistleblower can be in for trouble. Loyal employees who unmask unsavory things—be it that their colleagues submit padded expense accounts, misuse company property for private purposes, drink on the job, or indulge in other unappetizing behaviors—usually make themselves unpopular. Ostracism taken to the extreme of character assassination has been the fate in particular of women who dared to blow the whistle on sexual harassment. No matter that the unsuitability of the incriminating behavior was confirmed: those on the scene reacted in high dudgeon, taking umbrage at the "betrayal."

External whistleblowing is generally regarded as a disloyal act of denunciation, seldom as one of prevention to protect the community welfare. Where "my company, right or wrong" is nailed to the mast as the flag to which allegiance is due—out of misunderstood, because uncritical, loyalty—it may well happen that sounding the alarm in public is met with a summons to hand in your notice. Or else the powers that be bide their time until some other pretext can be dug up for terminating the dissenter. Instead of going into the urgent question of why the employee felt he or she had no other choice than to take the extremely distasteful (for the company) step outside, and then setting about to deal with the problem exposed, often everything is centered on ostracizing the person who let the side down.

An empirical sounding of American employees' attitudes to whistle-blowing yielded some interesting findings.[31] There is a recognized sequence that should be hewn to. First, try every possible internal channel, and only when this avails nothing, call in the law and then—last of all—the media. Whistleblowing tends to be more readily accepted in connection with illegal than with unethical conduct. It is widely believed that whistleblowers run a big risk of losing their jobs and should therefore enjoy protection at law.

A "Manual" for Whistleblowers

There is no shortage of articles that discuss in detail how someone who is faced with a moral problem in an institution ought to proceed. The spectrum of possibilities is very broad indeed:

---

31. E.S. Callahan and J.W. Collins, "Employee Attitudes Toward Whistleblowing: Management and Public Policy Implications," in Journal of Business Ethics, vol. 11, no. 12 (1992): 939-948.

- Don't brood on it.
- Be an opportunist: go along with the ethically suspect behavior and learn to live with it.
- Lodge a protest.
- Play conscientious objector.
- Leave the company.
- Call attention to the situation anonymously.
- Or do it publicly.
- Threaten anonymously to expose the wrongdoing.
- Sabotage the practice or conduct perceived as unethical so as to block it.
- Parley with the people involved, working step by step to build an agreement on the corrective action to be taken.

Some of these responses are plainly dodges or cop-outs and simply immoral. Others do nothing whatsoever to further a good cause and are not worth serious consideration by the sincerely concerned whistle-blower.

A decision to leave the firm may alert the company to the existence of a problem and prod it into doing something about it. More likely, though, the signal will not be received or understood, and since—face it—most employees are replaceable, apart from whatever short-lived satisfaction the principled employee may feel, nothing further will happen.

Calling attention anonymously to something wrong can have the effect of triggering a change for the better while shielding the unknown whistleblower from reprisals. But it can also poison the work environment and eat away the relationship of personal trust among innocent bystanders, so to speak, that has existed up to then. Similar consequences ensue from the hardball version of this variant, namely threatening anonymously to go public.

Everything considered, talking it out with the people involved in an effort to reach agreement on an ethically defensible solution is the most expedient and advisable course of action. This direct approach offers the best promise of resolving the matter, and no one's reputation suffers. There is, of course, no guarantee that this will result in the desired changes, but it does bring the problem out into the open and gives everyone concerned a better chance to decide what should be done. And should all efforts to change things prove inconclusive and the whistle-blower be obliged to go public in the end, the good try will enhance the person's credibility.

Company employees need not acquiesce helplessly in suspected unethical practices by any means; they are definitely in a position to put up resistance and to set changes in motion. Only when all efforts prove fruitless and inaction would result in loss of life or unprofessional conduct would lead to untold misfortune—only then is there no choice left but to make the matter public. Had this happened before the Challenger tragedy or the Chernobyl catastrophe, a lot of grief and widespread economic fallout could have been averted. No employee owes it to an employer to keep mum about shady or unlawful goings on—about "designer" drugs made by a chemical company, to take an example. Loyalty and obedience to orders are binding only within the framework of the law. No institution, not even the church, let alone a business undertaking, can oblige a person to act against his or her conscience. A community that rode roughshod over conscience would infringe upon a personal human value, surpassing everything that any community may hold in common.

It may be that a company operates lawfully and in conformity with society's prevailing moral concepts, yet some employees find themselves unable to reconcile certain of its practices with what they feel is right— experimentation on animals, for instance. Their efforts to better the situation—in this case, by minimizing animal tests—are decidedly worthy of support. In the end, however, the only way for a troubled employee to get rid of such a problem may be to seek employment elsewhere.

Constructive Responses to Whistleblowing

Beyond any doubt, whistleblowing hits the target company extremely hard, most of all when it is held up to public exposure. As we may safely assume there will always be problems that can end in whistleblowing, it behooves every company to establish official channels open to everyone who has a well-founded and relevant criticism to register. This is the only way to amend unethical conduct without having to bring in outside parties. The corrections that need to be made can be brought about more speedily inside the company and at less cost and with less damage to a reputation. Moreover, loyal employees then have an inducement to go through internal channels.

In any event, the company should prevent a situation arising where an employee troubled by moral scruples sees no other recourse than to go public with them—this both in its own self-interest and out of responsibility toward the employee who, as we have said, may together with his or her family have to pay dearly for blowing the whistle.

An institutionalized complaints route can take various forms. Examples include leadership and teamwork guidelines that leave the way clear for a seriously motivated employee to take a problem step by step all the way up to the chairman of the board, internal ombudsman offices, and "I've got a problem" letter-boxes or phone numbers. Other possibilities are company-related but externally situated control persons or bodies, such as outside directors, courts of appeal, and the like. The crucially important thing is to see to it that an open but confidential accessway exists, making it possible to correct critical situations quickly while limiting the damage to everyone concerned.

The right way to deal with whistleblowing, then, is not to ignore or stigmatize those who see themselves compelled to speak out, but to make institutional provision for constructive responses to a very real dilemma. It should be part of every manager's or boss's job to periodically monitor any problems that have come up and their significance, the measures taken, and the results—all in the important interest of an ethical risk analysis.

It would also make sense to keep a watch out for recurrent "themes," with a view to eliminating structural weaknesses or defects. Those entrusted with ombudsman duties should be high enough up in the hierarchy to possess a degree of independence conferring immunity to browbeating or coercion. Furthermore, they must be free to go to top management if their own remedial efforts fail.

By giving an institutional form to whistleblowing, a company can also make it clear when it will not entertain grievances. Ralph Nader and others have suggested these exceptions:[32]

- when the supporting evidence is incomplete or facts have been misrepresented;
- where personal quarrels, petty resentments, or envy are behind the initiative, with the real motive being revenge;
- when monetary or other "rewards" are demanded in exchange for incriminating information (in a word, extortion); or
- when whistleblowing is used as a smokescreen in order to forestall justified dismissal.

In terms of establishing ombudsman offices, it is often argued that responsible superiors who can distinguish between right and wrong

---

32.   Nader, Petkas, and Blackwell, op. cit. 203ff.

should be able to nip ethical problems in the bud. The solution therefore lies in a germane personnel policy, not in the creation of new institutions. In principle this is correct—only it would seem that managerial paragons of the sort envisaged are not always to be found where they are needed at the time that they are needed. Even given optimal personnel policies, taking preventive institutional measures makes sense as a kind of safety net to mitigate avoidable spills.

PART IV

PERSONAL ETHICS AND HUMAN RESOURCES DEVELOPMENT

Every effort to upgrade the ethical quality of business operations with the help of corporate principles and all the good intentions invested in the establishment of ombudsman offices will come to naught so long as a company's employees—and notably those in management positions— themselves fall ethically short. To conclude from this that all you need to make further discussion superfluous is to entrust "good" people with leadership responsibility would be erroneous.

Personal ethics—that is, executives' character qualities, their social skills, their morals, and the way they handle power—are usually of paramount importance for a company. Chapters 17 through 20 analyze varieties of managerial behavior that avail neither commercial nor ethical goals—and hence the great importance attached to the selection and allround development of key personnel.

17. Envisioning Ideal Leadership

Business ethics would be an unrealistic exercise if it were to start from the "ideal" human being and with the paragon in mind proceed to marshal a hit parade of desirable characteristics, as it were. The character traits and moral concepts informing a business institution are no different from those in the world outside. Nonetheless, special regard should be paid to the professional and human qualities of the management cadre at the very least, because that is where people with a will to put corporate ethical precepts into practice are needed. Good will means being unreservedly ready not only to listen to others' arguments, but also to make what is recognized as good the basis of your own conduct and actions. This is not an unreasonable expectation, since we know for sure that such people do exist and moreover that they can positively influence the whole ethical climate in a company.

In their superiors, employees see a critical reference group for the ethical standards determining their own behavior. That is why a pathologically flawed influential individual—an Eichmann (ignorant administrator), a Richard III (calculated malice), or a Faust (using any means to get what one wants)—can wreak havoc throughout a company.

Venerable classical works advise us that expert knowledge and ability are a must for those who would lead, but that by no means do they suffice to make a leader. From time immemorial, the same composite of qualities has been demanded, almost longingly, of emperors, monarchs, commanders, rulers—and managers. It is worthwhile going back to these historical works—Lao Tzu's Tao and its power, the teachings of Confucius, the esoteric doctrines of the Upanishads, and Sun Tzu's The Art of War, describing the leader as intelligent, trustworthy, humane, courageous, and strict. Or to Plato's philosophy, which sees reason elevated to wisdom, justness, steadfastness, and circumspection as the cardinal virtues.

Max Weber goes further, notably in "Politics as a Vocation,[1]" which 80 years after it was written can still offer valuable pointers. All these writings give great importance to the so-called primary virtues: besides justness and courage, these include moderation and prudence, together with those core personal dispositions that can be described in terms of

---

1.   Max Weber, "Politics as a Vocation", *From Max Weber: Essays in Sociology,* translated and edited by H.H. Gerth and C. Wright Mills (New York: Oxford University Press, 1946) available online,
      http://www.ne.jp/asahi/moriyuki/abukuma/weber/lecture/politics_vocation.html

having the courage to stand up for your own convictions *(Zivilcourage)*, being a fair combatant, being tolerant, and having the ability to refuse obedience constructively. "Virtue" in this connection denotes more than a person's moral state of mind: virtuousness can only germinate in the context of an individual's interaction with others in a certain social setting.

By applying rigorous standards of selection, particularly to personnel in higher positions, and by promoting key people judiciously, a company can go some way toward ensuring that those who project it internally and externally exhibit certain qualities of character ("virtues") that do not deviate, in principle at least, from those defining the ideal type as described in the works just mentioned. Georg Enderle notes that leadership authority has three equally important sources—professional or technical competence, personality, and the position held:

> "A failure of ethical leadership can take place in any of the three and lead to far-reaching leadership problems. Want of professional competence can mislead into over-emphasizing the authority and overdoing the power to penalize that the position confers. A weak personality radiates too little charisma and is unable to create the trust needed to lead. If a leader is not given the authority his position calls for he cannot fully discharge his responsibility for fulfilling the company's objectives."[2]

It is not asking too much to wish for leaders endowed with the qualities of character that we would take for granted in people whose decisions our welfare and that of our families depended on. These would be people who are aware of their full responsibility for everything they do or fail to do and are moreover morally oriented. The morally oriented person is one who takes to heart the guiding values of his or her conduct and does the level best to live by them. By that criterion, people driven by an insatiable lust for power that can only be satisfied at the cost of harming their associates and their business fail to qualify as leaders, as do those whose character profile is defined by arbitrariness, self-righteousness, opportunism, and a lack of moderation. Selecting personalities who fit the leadership bill at every level of the hierarchy is not only important in the corporate perspective. Leaders with the right stuff are absolutely indispensable to a decentralization of authority.

---

2.   G. Enderle, *Handlungsorientierte Wirtschaftsethik. Grundlagen und Anwendungen* (Bern: Paul Haupt, 1993), 127f.

The secondary virtues deserve a few words too. These virtues encompass ideals and attitudes like loyalty, diligence, uprightness, thriftiness, dependability, punctuality, and, yes, a liking for orderliness— precisely the virtues that were behind the success of the early industrial revolution in Europe and North America and that have been the driving force of the Asian threshold countries' economic surge in our time.

When it is a question of maintaining international competitiveness and of securing an industrial position, precisely then are secondary virtues indispensable, albeit with this incontestable proviso: only in combination with the primary virtues can these prove to be a blessing.

It is imperative that we give those "old-fashioned" values a rethink, most compellingly with an eye to matching the upcoming Asian countries, for example, whose peoples are remarkable for their industry, discipline, training and education, and modest demands. When people only give thought to what they have coming to them but forget what they must do to earn it, they fall short of a primary virtue: fair and upright dealing. Then not only does competitiveness slacken and unemployment spread, but in the end the whole society degenerates.

Max Weber pointed out that nobody has the right to take goodness and perfection in others for granted; we always have to reckon with "people's average flaws."[3] Although that admonition is well taken, it is still worthwhile to consider how the "ideal" leader might look. After all, if we do not even try aiming for the ideal, we end up with the mediocre or worse. In his lecture "Politics as a Vocation," Weber describes the three qualities that are decisive for politicians: passion, responsibility and proportion.[4] They are no less important in the business world, for there too executive responsibility is a "political profession." Weber relates the three qualities to each other thus:

> "To be sure, mere passion, however genuinely felt, is not enough.
> It does not make a politician, unless passion as devotion to a
> 'cause' also makes responsibility to this cause the guiding star of
> action. And for this, a sense of proportion is needed. This is the
> decisive psychological quality of the politician: his ability to let
> realities work upon him with inner concentration and calmness.
> Hence his distance to things and men. 'Lack of distance' *per se* is
> one of the deadly sins of every politician. It is one of those
> qualities the breeding of which will condemn the progeny of our

3.   Max Weber, "Politics as a Vocation," op. cit.
4.   Ibid.

intellectuals to political incapacity. For the problem is simply how can warm passion and a cool sense of proportion be forged together in one and the same soul? Politics is made with the head, not with other parts of the body or soul. And yet devotion to politics, if it is not to be frivolous intellectual play but rather genuinely human conduct, can be born and nourished from passion alone. However, that firm taming of the soul, which distinguishes the passionate politician and differentiates him from the 'sterilely excited' and mere political dilettante, is possible only through habituation to detachment in every sense of the word. The 'strength' of a political 'personality' means, in the first place, the possession of these qualities of passion, responsibility, and proportion."[5]

In the subsequent passage Weber talks about vanity, a foible we all have. In its triviality he sees an "all too human enemy: a quite vulgar vanity, the deadly enemy of all matter-of-fact devotion to cause and of all distance ... towards one's self." For Weber, "sin against the lofty spirit" of one's vocation begins where striving for power

> "... ceases to be *objective* and becomes purely personal self-intoxication, instead of exclusively entering the service of 'the cause.' For ultimately there are only two kinds of deadly sins in the field of politics: lack of objectivity and—often but not always identical with it—irresponsibility. Vanity, the need personally to stand in the foreground as clearly as possible, strongly tempts the politician to commit one or both of these sins."[6]

We hardly need to add that the same applies to more than just politicians in the narrow sense of the word. Some years ago the Club of Rome sent out a call for new leaders with a new profile.[7] They should have the ability to:

- develop strategic visions;
- act innovatively and adapt to change;
- develop ethical perspectives;
- take decisions and see to it that they are implemented;
- learn;
- change their opinion as they gain deeper insight into situations and problems;

---

5. Ibid.
6. Ibid.
7. Club of Rome (ed.), *Die Globale Revolution. Bericht des Club of Rome* 1991.

- treat strategic and tactical considerations as means, not ends; and
- establish systems serving to keep them informed about what people around them need, fear, demand, and suggest.

Rupert Lay emphasizes the ability to be a team player, which means, among other things, arriving at consensus through learning together with others. Another qualification is adaptability, which presupposes the ability to apprehend social facts and conditions and respond to them appropriately. Conflicts should be had out with a reasonable (measured by the result) expenditure of time and energy and be settled at the right moment. For this, besides being in command of the requisite techniques, leaders must have the ability to handle their own fears and those of others sensibly. Tolerance, particularly toward opinions that deviate from the "norm" and of people who enjoy no one's sympathy, is a further key leadership quality on Lay's list.[8] And to round it off, let us mention the ability to be passively active—meaning to listen, observe, wait, reflect, and be patient—as contrasted with having a one-track focus fixated on fighting, winning, and having your own way.

In the hustle and bustle of public and business life, we too seldom practice "mind training through attentiveness," as commended by the great German Buddhist Mahathera Nyanaponika:

> "Much of the world's suffering arises not so much from deliberate badness as from thoughtlessness, heedlessness, rashness and lack of self-control. Just one moment's pause to reflect would often suffice to prevent a far-reaching concatenation of disaster or wrong."[9]

Wherever there is an effort to translate ethical precepts into business practice, the "professionalism" of those who lead should be defined holistically. Over and above economic expertise and the ability to think equitably and be a responsible caretaker of entrusted corporate resources, specific quality-hallmark traits of character and ways of behaving also loom large. We will turn to these now.

Among the most important qualities demanded of those who lead is social competence, or what might be called "sociability"—meaning the ability to empathize, to be outside your own skin, and to respect other people as human beings irrespective of your current interests or where

---

8.   R. Lay, *Kommunikation für Manager* (Düsseldorf: Econ, 1989), 131ff.

9.   M. Nyanaponika, *Geistestraining durch Achtsamkeit* (Konstanz: Verlag Christiani, 1984), 35f.

they stand in the hierarchy. So construed, social competence is not at all the same thing as soft-hearted permissiveness that puts up uncritically with poor work performance, sloppy discipline, or other job-related dereliction. Nor is it the other, autocratic extreme of treating people as pawns on a utilitarian chessboard.

Social competence is already evident in the niceties of behavior we call good manners, the genuine article being inborn tact. Both qualities seem to have gone out of fashion. Nowadays, ostentatiously "cool" uncouthness, crass impertinence, or subtler forms of disrespect appear to be the behavioral models that pampered young tigers—and, come to that, superannuated Yuppies too—find most worthy of emulation for convincing themselves and others of their importance and indispensability. Certainly civility and courtesy cannot be ordered up on demand, but they can and should be instilled because they are, as Hans Jonas puts it, preconditions of civilized social interaction.[10] Even though "good form" in our associations with others has nothing to do with morality as such or with goodness or nobility, the appearance it grafts onto the raw "truth," and even the dissembling it ritualizes, functions as a vital lubricant that smoothes over the internal frictions of the social machinery's infrastructure, lodged in interpersonal relations, freeing the actors to step out into the suprapersonal public sphere and there to discharge their collective responsibilities.

How competent social competence really is comes out notably in the extreme case, when employees have to be let go. First and foremost it is imperative to sustain their self-worth true to the Golden Rule: Always behave in such a way that if roles were reversed you would accept the same treatment. Never should a leader lose sight of the fact that many employees are people who have been with the firm for most of their adult lives, whose work is their lifeblood, and who may identify more closely with the company than many a young MBA in a managerial chair. Not only are they torn away from long-familiar surroundings; they also suffer a blow to their security, their income, and their status in the eyes of their colleagues and society.

Before deciding to let someone go, the personal impact should therefore be considered just as carefully as the company's gain. If redundancies are unavoidable, they should be carried out in a socially tolerable fashion and made as bearable as possible with the help of

---

10. H. Jonas, "Zur Bedeutung von Sitte," in H. Jonas and D. Mieth (eds.), *Was für morgen lebenswichtig ist. Unentdeckte Zukunftswerte,* 4th ed. (Freiburg i.Br.: Herder Verlag, 1988), 10f.

internal job transfers, re-education programs, and, as a last resort, outplacement assistance rather than simply dismissing people with the curt explanation that the business situation leaves no other choice. Capital and labor, though legally equal production factors, are not of equal value ethically. People's welfare and a decent concern for their purity are ethically of greater worth than adding to capital assets. Given this scale of values, top management is duty-bound to strike a fair balance between the two production factors.

Although it may sound antiquated and at odds with the prevailing weather, it is important to recall that loyalty and readiness to take on responsibility are based on reciprocity. The employee owes the employer the same measure of constructive commitment as the company does the employee. If people who have a job and are paid well for doing it give less than they could, if they mishandle the assets and discretionary authority entrusted to them or even line their pockets at the expense of the business, then social competence also entails penalizing such behavior, up to and including dismissal.

Socially inept people—the "hard-nosed" boss types who put on airs and are high-handed, cynical, cold, or irascible with their employees, who get a kick out of hurting others or giving them the brush-off, all ostensibly in aid of what's best for the firm—are not only bad news humanly speaking. They are also plainly and simply bad managers. Superiors who make ciphers of their subordinates overlook the fact that they themselves are the original noughts. Coaching, in the sense of helping employees and colleagues to achieve their goals with an eye to the overall picture; arriving at decisions collectively and communicatively; giving voice to solutions-directed criticism constructively and objectively (boosting, not berating); keeping a strict separation between the matters at issue and emotions in interpersonal conflicts—all these have a bearing on ethics in the business world, and more: they also have much to do with effective management, because motivated, satisfied people outperform sat-upon, maltreated employees.

Managers with a "Pontifex Maximus" complex, who, imagining themselves in possession of the eternal truth, proclaim the same and are impervious to constructive criticism, also pose an in-house problem with ethical repercussions. These are mostly people who equate their position in the hierarchy with some higher quality on the scale of humanity. With their delusions of self-importance they are capable of—for example— sacking workers when costs must be slashed or hardlining it in pay negotiations while at the same time taking for granted the perks that go with their eminence (personal assistants, company car and driver) or, if shown the door because of proven incompetence, their right to a golden parachute.

A social behavior and power posturing may help the offending party to forget momentarily the garbage festering in his or her soul and to cover up the hollowness within. But hardly anyone is impressed—not for long, anyway. And deep down inside, those who act thus have an inkling that their overbearing ways are misbegotten—one telling indication being that when done unto as they have done unto others for years on end, they generally react with consternation and tearful chagrin.

18. Instead of Group Think, Zivilcourage

Civil courage however can only grow out of the free responsibility
of free men.
Dietrich Bonhoeffer[11]

There is no exact equivalent in English of the German word *Zivilcourage*. It translates literally as "civil (or civic) courage." Descriptively, it means having the courage of your own convictions and values and standing up for them, even and indeed especially when the social milieu espouses other convictions and values. It means not being afraid to fight for what, after judicious reflection, a person holds to be right and true, whether to the liking of those in a position to bestow favors and support or not. The fact that *Zivilcourage* can provoke unpleasant retaliation from "on high" is inherent in the definition—otherwise no courage would be required. The Socratic image of the ideal leader, as described by Plato, morally justifies prodding others to act. Corporate gadflies are obviously as unwelcome as the corporate complainer or, in extreme instances, the whistleblower. Yet the value of the devil's advocate to prevent "groupthink" resulting in corporate fiascoes becomes somewhat more respected when the facts are known.

According to Irving Janis, groupthink occurs when the members of a highly cohesive group allow their feelings toward the group to distort their individual capacity to reason. In other words, group processes interfere with individual reasoning. What happens, according to Janis, is that a consensus on the issue of discussion emerges within a group. This

---

11. Dietrich Bonhoeffer, "Prisoner for God", in *Letters and Papers from Prison by Dietrich Bonhoeffer*, ed. by Eberhard Bethge, transl. by Reginald H. Fuller (New York: The Macmillan Company 1960), 16.

consensus is then protected from critical appraisal by collective rationalizations, self-censorship, a group pressure on deviants to conform, and the emergence of "mindguards" who protect the group consensus by attacking adverse information. When groupthink occurs, it produces assessments based on stereotyped views of opponents as weak, evil, or stupid. It also leads to an unexamined faith in the group's inherent ability and morality and to a shared illusion of invulnerability. As a result, members of the group approach problems simplistically and fail to look critically at their deliberations and beliefs.[12]

This experience is not unique to corporations. As has become glaringly evident since 1989, it was at least as widespread in the former East Bloc. There, too, groupthink and lack of *Zivilcourage* led to disasters that need not have happened. Describing his impressions, Vittorio Hösle writes of how people

> "pretended to accept certain principles that in their heart they had long since cast off, and this knowing full well that their partners in dialogue also rejected them. Nevertheless one had to chime in with communication rituals...where all solemnly averred to one another the truth of those principles and where everyone knew, but no one said, that the emperor was naked." [13]

Joachim Gauck put his life experiences as an opponent of the former German Democratic Republic in a nutshell: "Breeding of underlings can be done" and "Well-tried means of achieving breeding success are the use of fear and the instruments of power by a power center that arrogates all possible authority to itself, and obscuring where power really resides by laying down an organizational smoke screen...Naked mendacity can be spotted—deft rationalization, leveling down and trivialization are more efficient."[14] Resistance begins, Gauck ventured to suggest, with refusal of enthusiasm.

The summons to show more *Zivilcourage* resounds far beyond the political arena and the bounds of social systems. Analysis of all the major disasters of recent years shows that long before Three Mile Island, Chernobyl, the *Exxon Valdez* oil spill, or the sinking of the *Estonia* ferry, there were critical voices and warnings of weak points that in the event proved only too right. But the warning voices were unable to make

---

12. I.L. Janis, *Groupthink, Psychological Studies of Policy Decision and Fiascoes* (Houghton: Mifflin Company, 1982), 5f.

13. V. Hösle, *Philosophie der ökologischen Krise* (Munich: C.H. Beck, 1991), 21.

14. See ZEIT-Punkte No. 1 (1994): 7.

themselves heard. The meticulous postmortem performed on the Challenger disaster gives a particularly graphic picture of how easily, in a stress situation, compulsive patterns of thinking and acting can override plain scientific and technical facts. Had they been heeded, a tragic misdecision could have been averted.

Why was clearly formulated and extremely valuable information disregarded or not taken sufficiently into account? How can we prevent otherwise serious, well-informed, and intelligent people from sitting on their doubts in working groups and decision-making bodies and bowing to "groupthink" instead of bringing their full critical potential to bear? Who can explain why an atmosphere reminiscent of a tipsy stag party has the power to put the critical faculties out of action? The answers to these questions do not lie in barefaced manipulation by domineering superiors or the unbridled opportunism of subordinates alone. Entering into play are exceedingly subtle, self-imposed intragroup compulsions that the Alpha members, deliberately or not, reinforce. In addition, informal norms for maintaining friendly relations within the group evolve and become part of a tacit agenda.

What are the mechanisms of group dynamics that promote conformity and inhibit criticism? Janis depicts them thus: The group closes ranks against the "deviant" and steps up communication with him or her for as long as there is hope that he or she might yet fall in line. If this proves fruitless, communication with the renegade ceases abruptly. If the isolation tactic does not work either, then the odd person out is excluded step by step from further decisions in the interest of reestablishing group harmony.[15]

When loyalty to the group is elevated to the highest form of morality, no member any longer dares to bring up controversial topics or to call shaky arguments into question. A feeling of group invulnerability takes root, overblown optimism becomes rampant, and the inclination to take risks rises. The group's opinion is seen as self-evident; other viewpoints are written off. A self-appointed "mindguard," a zealot of subservience, works on potential or actual deviants, attempting to reintegrate them by the use of intimidation. In Eugen Drewermann's experience,

> "What he gives out as his own conviction is in reality nothing more
> than a radical version of the reference group's *common sense*...He
> is always several steps ahead of its goading demon—a

---

15. See I.L. Janis, op. cit.

> prophylactic chameleon whose fear of rejection drives him to
> identify most fiercely with those expectations of the others that
> promise the greatest reward if fulfilled. Over-fulfillment of
> certain group norms, originally impelled by fear of rejection, ends
> up as a means to coercion flaunted as a display pattern."[16]

In this kind of situation, people no longer cast independent or critical
votes. Instead, as George Orwell (castigating pompous verbiage) so
trenchantly put it, "like cavalry horses answering the bugle, [they] group
themselves automatically into the familiar dreary pattern."[17] The horses
already know how they have to form up; all they need is a signal.

Perfectly normal shortcomings can impair the quality of the decisions
that any group makes: human inadequacy, blinkered vision, fatigue,
emotional stress, misinformation or information gaps, and so on.
Groupthink is fraught with special dangers, however:

- Discussions, instead of ranging over the full spectrum of possibilities,
  are limited to considering just a few courses of action, often only one
  or the other.
- The objectives that really need to be achieved and their implicit
  worth fail to get re-examined.
- Nor is the plan of action that the majority initially leaned toward
  re-evaluated later on with an eye to possible lurking risks and hitches.
- The group members make little or no effort to pull in information
  from experts that could help them size up the costs and benefits of
  alternative courses of action.
- The group reacts selectively to facts and assessments, reserving its
  real interest for the facts and opinions that confirm the option the
  group favored to begin with.
- Group members spend little time identifying external factors that
  could thwart implementation of their plan. As a result, they neglect to
  work out the countermeasures or alternative scenarios that may be
  needed to keep things on course.

Janis sums up his core thesis in the form of a "law," namely: "The greater
the congeniality and the stronger the esprit de corps prevailing among
the members of a political decision-making body, the more acute is the

---

16. See E. Drewermann, *Kleriker. Psychogramm eines Ideals*, 8th ed. (Freiburg i.Br.,
    1990), 70.
17. G. Orwell, "Politics and the English Language" in G. Orwell, *Collected Essays*
    (London 1961), 337ff.; quoted in Erhard Eppler, *Kavalleriepferde beim Hornsignal.
    Die Krise der Politik im Spiegel der Sprache* (Frankfurt a.M.: Suhrkamp, 1992) 32.

danger that independent critical thinking will be supplanted by 'groupthink,' resulting in irrational and demeaning actions against outsiders."[18] Problems that nobody is happy with not only don't go away if ignored, they tend to get worse—a state of affairs that Albert Camus depicted graphically in *The Plague*. Collegiality and loyalty are all well and good, but there should also be room for cogent disagreement. Even simple institutional provisions such as that of *advocatus diaboli* that served the Roman Catholic church well over many centuries could help curb groupthink.

Stanley Milgram's famous experiments gave us striking evidence of what bondage to authority can lead to.[19] He selected volunteer subjects at random, soliciting their help in testing the (fictitious) "scientific" hypothesis that people's learning ability can be improved by punishing them each time they make a mistake. The so-called pupils (actors, but this the volunteers did not know) were tied to an "electric chair." The volunteer "teachers" were ordered to administer higher and higher shocks to the slow learners—concretely, (dummy) jolts going from 15 up to 450 volts—which they did. The actor-pupils screamed in desperation and begged to be released from further participation. Above a shock of 330 volts the pupils ceased to react at all. The greater the visual and acoustic distance from the learner victim, the more eager did the teachers show themselves to comply with potentially lethal orders. Conversely, the closer they were, the less they were disposed to obey.

A crucial revelation of the Milgram experiments was how spectacularly the sense of individual responsibility crumbles in a situation of hierarchic control. This, Milgram commented, "is perhaps the most fundamental lesson of our study: ordinary people simply doing their jobs, and without any particular hostility on their part, can become agents in a terrible destructive process. Moreover, even when the destructive effects of their work become patently clear, and they are asked to carry out actions incompatible with fundamental standards of morality, relatively few people have the internal resources needed to resist authority."[20] The stereotype defense that Eichmann notoriously recited at his trial in Jerusalem—"we were only doing our duty"—was heard in the Milgram study, too, in response to moral reproofs.[21]

---

18. I.L. Janis, op. cit. 13.
19. S. Milgram, *Das Milgram-Experiment. Zur Gehorhsamsbereitschaft gegenüber Autorität* (Reinbek bei Hamburg: Rowohlt, 1974).
20. Ibid. 145.
21. H. Arendt, *Eichmann in Jerusalem. Ein Bericht von der Banalität des Bösen*, 8th ed. (Munich: Piper, 1992).

From various occurrences where submission to authority led to ethical catastrophe, Milgram deduces a number of generally applicable lessons. In the context of business ethics, the following ones are important:

- There are always people who perform their job punctiliously but unreflectingly because their dominating principle is a functional rather than a moral one. In such people's minds, the sense of responsibility is inevitably shifted onto the commanding authority.
- Personal values such as loyalty, duty, and discipline derive from the hierarchy's technical requirements, and yet the individual perceives them as personal moral imperatives.
- Increased frequency of requests for "authorization" is an early warning sign that a subordinate suspects something is morally amiss.
- "Obedience" is not the outcome of a dramatic confrontation between two opposing wills. It is embedded in an encompassing milieu where social ties, career hopes, and routine technical procedures determine the whole tenor of life. The typical case is not the heroic figure who wrestles with his conscience or the pathologically aggressive person who ruthlessly exploits a position of power. The typical case is more likely to be the "functionary" who has been charged with a task and strives to awaken the impression that he is up to the job.

Milgram speaks of our capacity to abandon our humanity, "indeed, the inevitability that [man] does so as he merges his unique personality into larger institutional structures. This is a fatal defect that nature has built into us humans, and in the long run it leaves our kind with only a modest chance of survival."[22] He finds it ironic that the (secondary) virtues of loyalty, discipline, and self-sacrifice that we value so highly in the individual "are the very properties that create destructive organizational engines of war and bind men to malevolent systems of authority."

But an encouraging sociopsychological finding also came out of Stanley Milgram's project: not everybody obeys orders, even when threatened with severe punishment for disobeying. A persistent minority can trigger a snowball effect that sweeps up others in refusing to conform. *Zivilcourage* of this caliber—having the guts to act on your own moral beliefs, even and precisely when "all about you" are headed in another direction—calls for a high degree of battle-readiness.

---

22. S. Milgram, op. cit. 216.

In a company, systematic fostering of critical, levelheaded leaders who are also equipped with social intelligence and *Zivilcourage* helps to temper the risks of groupthink. Other means to the same end are flat hierarchies, empowerment, and regular use of "spoilsports" and devil's advocates, together with the appointment of different working groups to tackle the same problems under the leadership of top managers with whom they prepare, in a professional and nonpartisan spirit, various possible options for presentation to whatever body will make the final decision.

As already noted in our discussion of dialogue and consensus, steadfastness is an intrinsic part of *Zivilcourage*, and both are particularly significant in relation to "upstairs." The power gradient makes it easier to be steadfast in the direction of "downstairs" than to stand ground in the face of the throne. Wherever the management style has the effect of demotivating employees or even instilling fear in them, more than *Zivilcourage* will be crippled. So, too, will the ability of a company to learn from mistakes, since these will no longer be brought out into the open. From this it follows that not only *Zivilcourage* should be encouraged, but also a management style and hierarchical structures attuned to responding constructively to *Zivilcourage* rather than quashing it.

In *Politics as a Vocation*, Max Weber discusses the differences between two distinct ethical stances: conduct can be oriented to an "ethic of sentiment" *(Gesinnungsethik)* or to an "ethic of responsibility" *(Verantwortungsethik)*. About the former—the 'ethic of the Sermon on the Mount'—no further comment seems necessary; with regard to the latter Weber adds: one must be responsible for all predictable consequences of one's action. We are not concerned here with the theological problem whether Weber's interpretation of the Christian ethic is adequate. The problem for Weber is solely: can means justify ends—a problem which, in his view, the absolute ethic is unable to solve. The believer in an absolute ethic cannot stand up to the ethical irrationality of the world.[23] And yet, also for Weber, an absolute ethic *and* an ethic of responsibility are not totally antagonistic. They are complements, which together make up the man who is ripe for 'politics as a vocation.' Yet the distinction between them is of practical significance in business life. The extent of the ethics practiced in and by a company is measured not by the quality of the moral will behind it but by the practical results of what the company does.

---

23. Max Weber, *Gesammelte Politische Schriften* (Munich 1921), 443.

In the context of business, ethics by sentiment can be equated with an ethic of short-term commercial success, which says amen to anything and everything that contributes to sales or earnings. Company conduct based on the accountability ethic considers the effects on the environment, the community, and posterity, having a care for them all. This can entail self-restrictions with undesirable operative consequences. Yet a number of companies have practiced this ethic in exemplary fashion. Levi-Strauss, with its exceedingly fair and generous treatment of employees and its commendably firm stand, already referred to, on child and prisoner labor, is one of them. Novartis is another, with its very broad approach to corporate social responsibility.

Since Max Weber's time, further ethics of accountability have been set forth. Hans Jonas has formulated the most salient contemporary version.[24] Common to all of them is the emphasis placed on scrupulous evaluation of all the present and future consequences of a decision, particularly where ethical dilemmas are involved.

Is this asking too much? Is it unrealistic to call for such personalities, given the unlikelihood of finding them? We think not, because not only can people be positively challenged but, as Hannah Arendt said, they also prove capable, again and again, of acting positively in unexpected ways:

> "The decisive difference between the 'infinite improbabilities' on which all life on earth and everything natural really rest and the miraculous events that transpire in human affairs is, of course, that in the latter case there is a miracle worker whom we know— -that man seems in a most mysterious way to possess a gift for performing miracles. In everyday parlance we call this gift taking action."[25]

19. Handling Power

Power and authority are special forms of the social nexus—special in that the actors act within a hierarchy. In Max Weber's definition, power is every chance within a social network to assert one's will, even against opposition and regardless of what the chance hinges on.[26] It can hinge on force or other means, for example, concerning whose use the involved

---

24. H. Jonas, *Das Prinzip Verantwortung* (Zurich: Buchclub Ex Libris) 1987.
25. H. Arendt, "Freiheit und Politik," in H. Arendt, *Zwischen Vergangenheit und Zukunft* (Munich/Zurich: Piper, 1994), 222.
26. M. Weber, *Wirtschaft und Gesellschaft: Grundriss der verstehenden Soziologie*, 5th ed. (Tübingen 1980), 28.

parties need not be in agreement. Authority has a different face. To Weber, it signifies the opportunity to command compliance with a certain order from persons who can be designated.[27] In contrast to power, authority seeks legitimacy in one form or another, since it presupposes a material interest in its existence on the part of those subject to it. If this interest no longer applies, resistance can ensue in various guises: working to rule, playing coy with information, tacitly "laying down one's tools," and other forms of non-cooperation.

Nobody will dispute that authority is exerted in companies as well. But there, too, its *raison d'être* or its legitimacy depends on some sanctioning material or functional interest. This interest arises from the need to structure the company's overall operations into various sectors, with one person named responsible for each of them. Alongside this horizontal structuring, a vertical organization with superiors and subordinates is also necessary in order to coordinate the different sector activities, aligning them on the interests of the company as a whole. As a result, people depend on each other in a number of ways, and this translates into a network of authority that in its turn also requires legitimizing. The most critical point here is self-limitation, both downscale and up: legitimate power recognizes the rights of others. It therefore correlates with moral responsibility, conscientiousness, discipline, and social competence. Whoever has been entrusted with leadership responsibility also has duties and obligations to the people he or she leads. Since, however, a minimum of power is needed to get the right course of action implemented and to make ideas happen, it cannot be abolished completely.

Further essentials to putting in-house power relationships on a sound footing are leadership quality, professional competence, and a clear delineation of who has authority for what. If they are lacking or fall short, a company will not only be unable to operate efficiently and economically (not least because top remuneration and numerous privileges come with top positions), but the void will lead at some point to a flat refusal on the part of employees to fall in with or submit to authority.

In addition, it is essential to apportion power so as to foster and maintain individual creativity, innovative thrust, and initiative. If employees who have no power are regarded as ineffective and passive, this need not mean that they lack potential. It can well be the case that the "structural violence" emanating from unshared power has a crippling

---

27. Ibid.

effect, causing employees to sink into resignation. Where they are taken into decision-making processes, can take on responsibility, and also get to share in the profits of successful performance, a dynamics foreign to a slave economy is generated. Then employees are willing to make sacrifices when the going gets rough.

When they are listened to because management is convinced they have something important to say and where all important and relevant information and data are readily shared with them, the loyalty garnered has a quality that is missing where information policy is restrictive and privileged access to information is wielded as a tool of power. That is why an "objectification" of cooperative interpersonal relationships that does away with every trace of functionally unwarranted powerplay pretensions is absolutely imperative—not just from the ethical point of view, but from the business perspective as well.

Power Abuse and Mobbing

With few exceptions, every form of social super- and subordination goes back to an archaic power relationship that confers higher standing and greater social prestige on the higher-up. We find this nexus already prefigured in the pecking order that, as in a chicken run, frequently determines how members of groups get along together—starting with kindergarten, then in school, and on to life among colleagues in workshop and office.

In this connection, mobbing has come in for more and more attention in recent years. The difference between mobbing and "normal" conflicts in organizations is this: mobbing is a form of aggression usually perpetrated by several people and directed against a certain person, goes on for an extended length of time, is insidiously destructive rather than aboveboard, and ends by making the victim sick. Mobbing, together with cliquishness and the tolerated ostracizing of individuals or even whole departments, takes in every variety of contempt for fellow beings: insulting innuendo, spitefulness, bad-mouthing others behind their back, plotting and scheming, and groundless criticism, as well as systematic destabilization of colleagues that does not stop short of psychoterror.

Organization sociologist Norbert Paris has presented some important findings from his research on the subject.[28] The situation in many social and institutional settings is well known: there are opportunistic

---

28. N. Paris, "Dreierlei Schimpfklatsch. Über Dauergerede und Selbstverhetzung," in *Leviathan*, vol. 21, no. 4 (Opladen: Westdeutscher Verlag 1993).

troublemakers who seek to curry favor (with whomever) by hounding, spreading malicious gossip, and making underhanded digs against people looked upon as outsiders or has-beens. Paris shows that how people are esteemed or shunned has little to do with rational considerations and much to do with opportunism. It can even happen that a mischief maker will malign his intended victim for having the very qualities that those he is trying to impress regard as positive. There is small consolation in knowing that with their machinations the agitators themselves run a high risk, because "once power has been consolidated and the dirty work done, the people who are really in control have no qualms about dropping their party whips."[29]

Sexual harassment is a particularly despicable form of power abuse and one that has been largely passed over in European discussions of business ethics. Yet in a recent survey in Germany, 81 percent of the women queried complained of it.[30] American soundings also confirm its prevalence.[31] The range of what is defined as "sexual" and "harassment" varies from person to person; presumably the harassers define them differently than do the harassed. Given the difficulty of fixing the threshold beyond which harassment plainly occurs, it is advisable to stick to the rule of keeping more distance, not less, and when in doubt, don't. This relieves all concerned of the onus of trying to figure out exactly how far a person may or may not go.

Tearful laments over human iniquity and appeals to our better nature stand scant chance of changing things. There are more effective ways of confronting abuse of power and mobbing. First, strong signals must be sent down from the top echelon making it clear that offenders must, without exception, expect to incur severe sanctions. Anything and everything tantamount to intimidation, oppression, and other shows of contempt for human integrity and every form of discrimination due to age, sex, or race must be proscribed. Breaking down barriers to communication would also help considerably to improve the working atmosphere. In addition, ombudsman's offices are an important part of any effort to protect the "power disadvantaged," who normally have to overcome sizable hurdles when trying to assert their interests. The person in a secure position in the hierarchy, in contrast, notes Paris:

---

29. Ibid. 586.
30. R. Földy and O. Hill, *Das Mittelmässigkeits-Kartell,* op. cit. 69.
31. See K.A. Crain and K.A. Heischmidt, "Implementing Business Ethics: Sexual Harassment," in *Journal of Business Ethics,* vol. 14, no. 4 (April 1995): 299-308.

"has no need to get especially het up in order to assert his power....To stay on top, he who sits firmly in the saddle simply has to go on sitting. Since he does not aim for a change in the power structure, he only has to limit himself to passively cementing the status quo. He affects nonchalance and composure; an excess of fervor or verbose tirades would only serve to irritate, arousing the suspicion that perhaps the Man is not as sure of himself as he feigns to be."[32]

Power Abused for Personal Privilege

It is no secret that there are substantial differences between the topmost and lower-income brackets in companies. In discussions of these differences, it is often argued that very high salaries for top management are defensible, indeed crucial, because those who draw them have special abilities important to the company or are subject to extra-heavy pressures. Special treatment and privileges large and small add to their remuneration, starting with reserved parking spots, escalating with a chauffeured company car, expensive club memberships, and the like, and spinning out of control with freewheeling expense accounts and annual stock options that enable the beneficiary to clear his nominal salary several times over. These perks can only be contrived and carried into effect by the beneficiaries themselves, of course—a situation that has provoked increasingly frequent protests by critical shareholders in recent years.

While beauty may lie in the eye of the beholder, it is hard to understand either from an ethical standpoint or with a regard to fair apportionment of wealth why company heads should make $50 million a year—or even more than $200 million—when in the same companies jobs are being eliminated or paychecks slashed, allegedly because lagging profitability leaves no other choice. When particularly unscrupulous specimens of the high-roller genus milk the system with their company paid extravagances, not only are unjust income differences exacerbated, but company overheads also explode.

Let those who are bent on proving to themselves and others the superlative social status they enjoy by demonstrating to all and sundry that only the best food and drink in the best restaurants and other forms of conspicuous consumption are simply appropriate to their lifestyle go ahead and do so—only at their own expense. An infantile prestige

---

32. N. Paris, op. cit., 585.

complex or outmoded inner circle mind-set has no business being subsidized with company funds.

Where power of disposal over company resources is misused for private purposes or where personal indulgences are put down to business expenses, legal norms must be invoked and applied—if only for reasons of maintaining a clean operation. It is incomprehensible why a worker who "borrows" a tool for his hobby basement at home has usually to reckon with punishment up to getting sacked, while a highly placed and well-paid executive who lives it up with friends at a gourmet restaurant at company expense or squanders princely sums on business trips can count on tolerance because such is the done thing in the circles he or she moves in. And finally, a sense of fairness would suggest that the spotlight should also be turned on the excessively munificent golden handshakes and golden parachutes with which departing top managers are sped on their way, especially when crass mistakes in office have preceded their departure.

Admittedly, here as with every other instance of power abuse, black-and-white situations are more easily condemned than those containing gray areas. It is also understandable if in situations where there is room for doubt, a company prefers putting up with the odd transgressor to Stalinizing the whole system with a tight network of surveillance and controls. Nevertheless, where misdoing exists it must be got at; not only considerations of fair dealing but also the responsibility the company has to its shareholders dictate as much. Here again ethics and efficiency go hand in hand. Wrongly construed tolerance would send the wrong message, set skewed standards, and, once the everybody-does-it contagion had spread, lead eventually to an exorbitant cost avalanche.

20. All-Inclusive Human Resources Development

At first blush, it may not be readily apparent why a company should take on—in addition to job-related training and continuing education—the task of elementary moral education, which we would expect everyone to be equipped with by upbringing and schooling. All-inclusive personnel development can after all cost an organization quite a pretty penny. So if sins of omission in the matter of molding people to become moral beings have to be deplored, criticism would be better focused on earlier stages of human development—on family life and the education system, not on the business organization.

Is "morality" learnable at all? Answers to this question diverge. Immanuel Kant's was tinged with pessimism: "You cannot carpenter something straight and true from the twisted wood of which human beings are made."[33] Since his day, various schools of philosophy have repeatedly expressed skepticism regarding the moral ameliorability of man. Many hold that by the time of young adulthood, a person's education in moral discernment has for all practical purposes been concluded, which would mean that any later effort, no matter how well meant, to mold an ethical individual will have but an ephemeral and superficial influence at best. It is thus all the more to be deplored that the consultancy markets today teem with cash courses in "ethics." A once-over-lightly treatment can neither do justice to ethical problems in all their complexity nor bring about an improvement in the moral quality of people's actions. It only costs money that ends up in the hucksters' pockets. To be effective, an educational effort needs ample time.

As for including ethics in management development programs, there are both positive and negative reports.[34] Allround management development imparts, over and above the usual professional know-how, a grounding in ethics and fleshes it out with case histories. If a company's personnel and promotion policy is so conceived as to assure it of leaders invested with a "postconventional" (in Kohlberg's terminology[35]) level of judgement—people, that is, who do not submit blindly to existing rules and regulations but who form judgments based on morally defensible and responsibly weighed considerations—then that company can profit from the kind of management education just alluded to. This is not wishful thinking: empirical evidence supports the conclusion.

---

33. See I. Kant, "Ideen zu einer allgemeinen Geschichte in weltbürgerlicher Absicht," in W. Weischedel (ed.), vol. XI: *Schriften zur Anthropologie, Geschichtsphilosophie, Politik und Pädagogik I* (Frankfurt a.M. 1968), 41.

34. For positive reports, see e.g., D.R. Nelson and T.E. Obremski, "Promoting Moral Growth Through Intra-Group Participation," *in Journal of Business Ethics*, vol. 9. no. 9 (1990): 731-739. H.L. Johnson, "Bribery in International Markets: Diagnosis, Clarification and Remedy," *in Journal of Business Ethics*, vol. 4, no. 6, (1985): 447-455. For negative reports, see e.g. M.S. Lane, D. Schaupp, and B. Parsons, "Pygmalion Effect: An Issue for Business Education and Ethics," *in Journal of Business Ethics*, vol. 7, no. 3, (1988): 223-229. J.R. Davis, and R.E. Welton, "Professional Ethics: Business Students' perceptions," *in Journal of Business Ethics*, vol. 10, no. 6 (1991): 451-463.

35. L. Kohlberg, "Moral Stages and Moralization: The Cognitive-Developmental Approach," in Th. Lickona (ed): *Moral Development and Behaviour, Theory, Research, and Social Issues* (New York: Harper & Row, 1976), 31-53.

Practical Grounding with Case Studies

Moral philosophy today is so replete with theories of ethics that 'normal' people are more likely to lose than to find their bearings in the thicket. Each of the theories is based on a supreme moral principle, and in form they can be roughly classified as theological, teleological (consequential), or deontological (obligatory) ethics. Despite some fundamental differences between them, they all have some moral principles in common, at least as regards two basic valueconcepts: reason and justice.

Reason is not to be equated with intelligence. Though reason presupposes the latter, the chimpanzee that assembles two sticks to reach the banana also possesses intelligence. Reason, in contrast, is the ability to elaborate well-grounded ethical norms, to draw distinctions, and to develop value judgments that are just as valid as every other kind of judgment deriving from reason. On this premise, a reasonable decision would be one based on value judgments that all other reasonable persons accept as valid. The criterion of the justice or justness of a decision is fulfilled when the interests of everyone it affects have been given due consideration and its consequences for future generations and for the environment are morally defensible.

Attention needs first to be focused on these two criteria, reason and justice, as the keynotes of "basic morality" opening the way to the subject. If business decisions and guidelines are oriented toward these twinned moral principles, a good distance has already been traveled in the direction of a practicable business ethic. The actual content of this basic morality should be communicated through annotated "required reading" as homework, not through lectures on the various schools of philosophy since the pre-Socratics. Uplifting and intellectually challenging as they may be, set lectures are not suited to illustrating how the subject matter relates to actual workaday practice. Occasionally some film classics have didactic merit.

Working through case studies and discussing them together is especially useful. They can be of an abstract nature but also relate explicitly to business operations and ethical problems encountered in actual practice (rather than being simply entertaining, as it were). To be really effective learning tools, case studies should satisfy a number of requirements. Their quality and pedagogical value gain when they serve to bring out ethical dilemmas such as come up all the time in the complex workings of business and industry, thus ruling out facile black-and-white solutions. Case studies in which wrong decisions on public record (as in the Challenger disaster, for example) or in your own company are analyzed and the ethical ramifications pondered have great value. Likewise well-suited to the purpose are case studies that depict situations akin to that illustrated by the prisoner's dilemma (see Chapter 14), which demand decisions. Finally, case studies where a major business decision that turns out to be fraught with ethical minefields is taken apart and retraced can imprint the lesson that while single steps on the way to a final decision may be morally innocuous; their cumulative impact can prove problematic.

Case histories that come straight out of the company introduce realism by pointing up the potential borderline situations that can materialize in company operations. Wherever possible, the mistakes that were made and their consequences should be given a thorough going-over—in the spirit of Philip Johnson's "Business Ethics is an Inside Job."[36] Such self-scrutiny helps to prevent similar mistakes from happening again and adds credibility to efforts to learn from them.

Saul Gellerman plumbed the question of why "good" managers make "bad" ethical choices—decisions that turned out to be loaded with heavy liabilities for the companies concerned and in some cases even meant their ruin.[37] His findings show that there are four main misconceptions that lead executives astray:

- The belief that what they are doing is not "actually" unethical but falls just within the bounds of what is seemly and legal.
- The belief that what they are doing is in the best interests of someone or of the company—in other words, "they" somehow expect me to act thus.
- The belief that what one is doing is airtight, since no one will ever find out about it, let alone make it public.
- The belief that what one is doing helps the company, which will therefore turn a blind eye to it or, should it come to light, will cover the culprit.

Which kind of conduct is "only just" acceptable or where to draw the borderline between "clever" and overtly unethical conduct often remains unclear until the border is overstepped and a blunder committed. Yet in most cases, two simple questions put to the executive responsible would suffice to clear the ethical air beforehand:

36. P. Johnson, "Business Ethics Is An Inside Job," in *The Journal of Management Development*, vol. 11, no. 4, (1992): 44-48.
37. S.W. Gellermann, "Why 'good' managers make bad ethical choices," in *Harvard Business Review* (July/August 1986): 85-90.

- Could you give a plausible explanation of your decision to your family or a close friend without having to hem and haw or distort the situation?
- Would you feel comfortable if a newsmagazine or TV did an exposé 150 on it, inclusive of background and consequences?

If these questions cause the executive to start thinking twice, there is a strong possibility that something ethically fishy is afoot.

As for the second problematic "belief" cited by Gellerman, every company quite likely has a fund of concrete experience from which its employees can learn. His own experience in this connection is the "sad truth" that many a short-lived whiz gets promoted up the ladder and then—compounding the injustice of it all—some hapless successor is left to pick up the pieces. The lesson: unwontedly good results that defy explanation on the basis of the known circumstances ought always to be X-rayed with a view to finding out what is behind them.

Of the third fallacy on Gellerman's list, certainly always and everywhere some shady conduct goes undetected. For an ordinary mortal, a fancied low risk of being found out in combination with the lure of big personal gain could present a strong temptation. So Gellerman's advice is on the mark: Make it easier to detect wrongdoing. Stepped-up audits or spot checks without prior notice may suffice as deterrents. Prevention is better than cure or correction after the fact, and case studies could help clarify how this commonsense maxim might be applied in each company.

Finally, working with case studies can put paid to the notion that because a certain kind of immoral activity benefits it, a company should look the other way or even take the offender under its protective wing. In case studies—and, of course, above all in the mores actually practiced in a company—it should be made clear that loyalty to the firm comes up against its limits when the rights of others are trampled on.

In the course of working through case studies together, a fringe benefit almost always emerges: preconceived ideas that colleagues have had about each other are amended. Surveys show time and again that people believe they themselves have a moral edge over most of their colleagues.[38] And among female managers, the (as yet) unproved opinion

38. G.M. McDonald and R.A. Zepp, "Ethical Perceptions of Hong Kong Chinese Business Managers," *in Journal of Business Ethics*, vol, 7, no. 11, (1988): 835-845; O.C. Ferrel and K.M. Weaver, "Ethical Beliefs of Marketing Managers," *in Journal of Marketing*, vol. 47, (July 1978): 69-73; L.F. Pitt and R. Abratt, "Corruption in Business: Are Management Attitudes Right?" *in Journal of Business Ethics*, vol. 5, no. 1, (1986): 39-44.

is widespread that women are morally superior to their male peers.[39]

Intercultural Management

Outside their homeland, multinational corporations come up against all kinds of differences—in social customs, educational backgrounds, technology, and culture. (See Chapter 2.) This otherness demands a special knack from the executive assigned to take on management responsibility in a foreign country. Only very obtuse, ethnocentrically fixed, or exceptionally stupid people will refuse to accept that what other cultures and their intellectual elites have to offer can be a source of fresh impulses, modifying a person's own outlook on and way of doing things. But the culture gap can also be a source of latent misunderstandings and problematic confrontations.

One usage that constantly causes problems is the often excessive— from a Western viewpoint—loyalty shown to the family or kin group, with the effect that decisions having to do, for example, with purchases or personnel or investment project siting and so on are made more with an eye to what is best for family or clan rather than for the company. Differences in the value attached to time, though less consequential, can also prove bothersome. The Germans and Swiss are generally regarded as being clock-hound zealots of punctuality, whereas Africans move in a different time frame. Where being on time or not depends on age and status, subordinates are expected to appear on the dot, with the prerogative of showing up late reserved for higher ups or elders. This is not conducive to efficient programming.

To deal correctly with unfamiliar cultures, it is of course very important to know something about their traditional values and norms and also to be able to empathize with sometimes completely different ways of looking at the world that determine how people perceive, judge, and act. Culturally determined elements all have an influence on how people visualize reality and communicate their views. Communication has to do with much more than a local or tribal language or dialect; as an interchange of information and feelings, it takes place on both the cognitive and the emotional level. Not only the content but also the message thus gets its meaning from how it is conveyed.

---

39. S.W. Kelley, O.C. Ferrell, and S.J. Skinner, "Ethical Behaviour Among Marketing Researchers: An Assessment of Selected Demographic Characteristics," in *Journal of Business Ethics*, vol. 9, no. 8, (1990): 681-688.

And interpersonal communication is irreversible: once something is said, it cannot be taken back. You can perhaps try to explain in more detail or to differentiate or relativize, but you cannot delete what you later wish you had not said. A European manager who sharply contradicts an Asian in the presence of other Asians or otherwise breaches culturally rooted rules commits a rudeness that can be put right only with great difficulty, if at all. For all these reasons, it is important to recognize the cultural dimension of verbal and nonverbal communication, in relation both to yourself and to people from other cultures.

It would be too much to expect executives of transnational concerns to turn themselves into anthropologists or experts in intercultural understanding. Nevertheless, managers working in a culturally confluential environment do have to satisfy quite high personal requirements. In addition to handling the problems that normally come up in their work, they must be capable of thinking themselves into all sorts of roles and standpoints, some of which may differ greatly from their own, but without relinquishing their power to act. They must also be able to deal with frustrations and conflicts stemming from culturally conditioned misunderstandings—unfulfilled expectations, unkept promises, fully unexpected disappointments—deftly enough to clear the air of pentup resentments.

To underscore the point: the fact that colleagues, friends, superiors, or customers come from a culture that differs from our own definitely does not mean that they are uncultivated. To stamp them as "underdeveloped" because they come from an economically underdeveloped country is not acceptable from either a business or a business ethics viewpoint. Intercultural tolerance and the kind of understanding it demands can be awakened by giving due place to the crosscultural aspects of the international executive profile in management development programs.

CONCLUSIONS: THE WAY AHEAD

By three methods we may learn wisdom: First, by reflection,
which is noblest;
Second, by imitation, which is easiest; and third by experience,
which is the bitterest.

Confucius

From an ethical point of view it is desirable for companies, as *corporate citizens* of both local and global society, to see that the principles laid down in the Universal Declaration of Human Rights are acted on within their sphere of influence, to show "good" and "fair" behavior in terms of putting socio-ethical and eco-ethical standards into practice, and—where the only deficit that might remain is in "legal" behavior—to create legitimacy through a redoubling of efforts. Since illegal or illegitimate entrepreneurial activity is not only morally unjustifiable but also often causes avoidable and in some cases substantial damage both to humans and to the environment, options for action based on ethical judgments are preferable to all other possible kinds of action.

First Things First: It's the Right Thing to Do.

When irregularities become apparent, then the question of whether or not corrective action should be taken is not an issue for companies and managers with an ethical sense of legitimacy. Since they also want moral recognition for their actions, the (re)-establishment of legitimate conditions is the only justifiable way forward. Corrective action is taken in its own right; *it is the right thing to do.* Through the cultivation of a corporate culture informed by ethical judgments and through the on-going effort to live this culture in the day-to-day routine, the likelihood of illegitimate activity is kept to a minimum. A company of this kind gives categorical priority to ethical aspects and—in enlightened and intelligent self-restraint[1]—avoids any morally ambivalent business. Where this leads to added costs, sales penalties, loss of market share, the need for additional investment and thus ultimately to lower operating profits, or where "ethics" does not "pay off" in some other way, this is accepted out of the conviction that, as a matter of principle, illegitimate activity is not an option.

In addition to observing the existing laws, international codes of conduct and national regulations, such companies will also engage in

---

1. See Maak Th., "Republikanische Wirtschaftsethik als intelligente Selbstbindung," *Beiträge und Berichte*, no. 81 (St. Gallen: Institut für Wirtschaftsethik, 1998).

dialogue with critical stakeholders. They do this to remain sensitized to respect for the rights of others and to test their own claims for recognition through a discourse focused on the achievement of consensus. For the same reasons—and because human weaknesses are known to be a part of human existence, and activities which in the past were deemed morally acceptable may need to be corrected in the light of new insights—these companies create a corporate culture which is open to criticism. Where internal corporate dialogue leads to the company steering the right course, this is appreciated and promoted as an internal learning experience. Behavior patterns of this kind are overall the best way of dealing with problems because they are proactive and constructive.

A different—but not mutually exclusive—argument is that ethically legitimate corporate activity in the long term is also of advantage in business terms.

The "Business Case" of Business Ethics

Companies which for intrinsic reasons do the "right thing" may encounter incomprehension and rejection in an environment with a one-sided focus on monetary quarterly results: Whereas the "costs" of such efforts can in most cases quite clearly be quantified as additional costs (training of employees, communication of guidelines, improvement in social security systems or environmental protection) and possibly also as a renunciation of sales, any business advantage that may arise, the "return on ethical investment" is only measurable in the short term in very rare cases, if at all.

The avoided cost of accidents, strikes, public criticism or additional political regulations is just as unsusceptible to measurement as the environmental damage which does not occur because of investments made to prevent it. Share prices, too, can usually be explained more by general bullish or bearish movements on the US American markets and sector-specific preferences than by the moral quality of specific corporate activity. Although one could argue with reference to concrete cases such as Enron, WorldCom, Tyco or others that "if you think compliance with ethical criteria is expensive, try non-compliance", it would be dishonest not to concede the problems of measuring the success of ethically legitimate corporate activity.

There is, however, evidence which is plausible and needs to be taken seriously that good corporate ethics not only has intrinsic value, but also—at least in the long term—leads to measurable advantages for the company[2] and the national economy.[3] At least the following conscious efforts to put ethical judgments into concrete practical actions of constructive dissent management are known today to offer (medium-term and long-term) strategic corporate advantages—the *"Business Case"*.

Prevention or Reduction of Costs of Friction with the Social Environment

Where corporate behavior comes to light which is perceived to be illegitimate, whether it is illegal or legal, this leads to frictions with the social environment and thus to a damaged reputation: Whether a critically engaged public demonstrates in front of the factory gates, aid organizations erect "wailing walls" or the media exert pressure through critical reporting—for the company concerned this means a lessening of social acceptance. Whether the share prices fall or concrete measurable sales penalties are suffered as a result of this or not is of secondary importance. External criticism means that management capacity has to be committed for defensive activities and the "heads" are thus not free to make use of opportunities on markets and to help shape the future. Where the impression also arises that the reprehensible "Goliath" is treating the innocent "David" in an inhuman manner, a company loses a great deal of sympathy, which can only be regained at great cost.

By contrast, the evidence is accumulating that the standing of a company is becoming a competitive advantage, because a positive coefficient is generated in the form of sympathy and affinity. This becomes a decisive market advantage that is empirically measurable in those cases where a company sells products and services which are comparable in quality and usefulness with those of other companies *(me-too products)*.[4] An ethical corporate identity that enjoys positive associations in society confers on products an added benefit which ethically sensitive consumers consider when deciding which products to buy.[5]

---

2. Garone St.J., *The Link Between Corporate Citizenship and Financial Performance—Research Report* (New York: The Conference Board, 1999); R.M. Roman et al., "The Relationship between Social and Financial Performance—Repainting a Portrait," in *Business & Society*, vol. 38, no. 1, (1999): 109-125.

3. See Amartya Sen and his conclusion that, despite all deep-seated ambiguities and the complexity inherent in the problem, the reward of ethical behaviour is quite considerable, in A. Sen, *On Ethics and Economics* (Oxford: Blackwell, 1987).

4. L. Sharp Paine, "Managing for Organizational Integrity," in *Harvard Business Review* (March-April 1994).

5. P. Pruzan, "Corporate Reputation: Image and Identity," in *Corporate Reputation Review*, vol. 4, no. 1, (2001): 50-64.

An integrated definition of responsibility towards the customer brings just as much advantage as the responsibility shown in respect of the products: the consumer normally rewards it.[6] Conversely, sports shoes and fashionable sportswear offer examples of how people vote with their purchasing power when they perceive corporate activity to be illegitimate— and internet sites are available to help in the decision-making.

Motivation of Employees and Competitive Advantage on the Jobs Market

If a company acts in an illegitimate manner and bullies decent people who are simply doing their social duty to prevent avoidable damage to third parties, then as a rule this also has negative effects on company morale and job satisfaction.[7] In the medium to long term, this can lead to employees whose talents and quality-mindedness are of value to the company looking around for job opportunities with other companies *("exit")*. But since talented employees today are seen as the most valuable asset of a company, unethical behavior also from this point of view cannot be seen to lie in the interest of the company. Evidence suggesting that for the best graduates from universities the good reputation of their future employer plays a major role in their choice of company to work for is also to be seen in this connection.[8] Where corporate behavior is perceived as ethically correct, job satisfaction and the identification of employees with their company increase in a good working atmosphere. Both have a measurably positive effect on company results, not only in Western Europe and the USA, but also among newly industrialized countries (NICs) in Asia.[9]

---

6.   One of the best examples is probably the consumer behaviour in the cases of the analgesic "Tylenol", which was withdrawn completely from the shelves by Johnson & Johnson because of isolated deliberate contamination by blackmailers and was re-launched just months later with great success in completely new tamper-proof packaging; see C. Canon, "Tylenol's Rebound," in *Los Angeles Times*, Part 1, (September 25): 16.

7.   Hian Chye Koh and El'fred A.Y. Boo, "The Link between Organizational Ethics and Job Satisfaction: A study of managers in Singapore," in *Journal of Business Ethics*, (vol. 29, no. 4): 309-324; in Singapore it were above all three factors which played a role: The support of top management for ethical behaviour, the "ethical climate" in the organization and the link between ethical behaviour and career success.

8.   D. Bradshaw, "Family values replace the dash for cash," in *Financial Times*, (May 25th, 1998); also T. Larsen and M. Sørensen, "Top Leaders boycott unethical companies," in *Borsens Nyhedsmagasin*, no. 1, (2001): 14ff; and P. Pruzan, "Corporate Reputation: Image and Identity," in *Corporate Reputation Review*, vol. 4, no. 1, (2001): 53f.

9.   Hian Chye Koh and El'fred A.Y. Boo, op. cit.

Motivation of employees increases where applied business ethics, including constructive dissent management, becomes an integral part of a company's "moral corporate identity", which as cultural totality of the values, patterns of thinking and decision-making, modes of behavior and structures within the company gives employees a positive sense of "us". People are committing themselves to something in their working life with which they can also fully identify at a personal level, and which they can talk about with pride among family and friends. Motivated employees will achieve more than those who feel compelled to do their "job" for economic reasons. What Jacob Burckhardt once said with regard to individuals also applies for whole companies: They are not simply what they are, but they are also that which they have set as their ideal. Even if they do not fully match up to this ideal, a part of their being is nevertheless defined by this naked ambition to achieve.[10]

Attractiveness of the Company for Ethically Minded Investors
In spite—perhaps even because—of the discussions on shareholder value (however this might be defined[11]) which have been unleashed by recent cases of corporate fraud and "creative accounting", companies today are no longer measured exclusively by what they produce, but also by what they represent. There are periodicals that deal with "best practices" in the context of the "ethical performance" of companies[12] and thus set transparent benchmarks for competitors in this regard. Such practices are becoming increasingly important, because there is a substantial and growing number of pension funds and other institutional investors which do not only look at short-term yields, but also at the way in which these yields are achieved.[13] Estimates on the financial power of ethically minded investors are put at more than 2000 billion dollar—about 13 percent of the 16,300 billion dollars accounted for by professional investors.[14] In the case of a business performance that in other respects is equally good, investment sums in this order of magnitude can make a significant difference for the share price.

10. J. Burckhardt, "Griechische Kulturgeschichte," cited in A. Riklin, *Politische Ethik— Vorträge der Aeneas-Silvius-Stiftung an der Universität Basel* (Basel: Helbing & Lichtenhahn, 1987).
11. A. Brink, *Holistisches Shareholder-Value-Management* (Munich: Rainer Hampp Verlag, 2000), 95ff.
12. *Ethical Performance—Best Practices,* obtainable from publisher@ethicalperformance.com.
13. For discussion of the criteria, see C. Mckenzie, "The Choice of Criteria in Ethical Investment," in *Business Ethics—A European Review,* vol. 7, no. 2, (April 1998): 81-86.
14. P. Pruzan, "Corporate Reputation: Image and Identity," op. cit. 52.

American management consultants such as Charles Fombrun (Reputation Institute[15]) estimate that up to 30 percent of shareholder value is attributable to the good reputation of a company—other estimates[16] are considerably more conservative. It is a proven fact that there are companies that achieve outstanding results both in business and in social and ecological terms.[17] "Ethical investment funds" are also producing results on the equity markets that are at least no worse than those of funds that apply broader investment criteria.[18] Both provide evidence underlining the business compatibility, at least in the medium to long term, of ethically legitimized corporate activity.[19]

The reputation of a company, defined as the sum of perceptions of all stakeholders, is a complex construct and in most cases the result of many years' hard work. It can be jeopardized by just a few determinedly inadequate actions. When prime time television shows members of top management being led off in handcuffs, "business" problems are of secondary importance. And when a company first appears on the "Ten Worst Corporations" list published each year by US American corporate critics such as Russel Mokhiber and Robert Weissman or in the publications of "Corporate Crime Watch"[20], immense problems of legitimacy and standing emerge, with direct consequences on the product markets, regardless of whether the internal corporate perception corresponds to the external perception or not. Even the Stoic philosophers of Ancient Greece pointed out that it is not facts that unsettle people, but opinions about facts. So-called "critical shareholders"—represented today in a global umbrella organization— make sure that unethical corporate activity can be addressed today, if need be even directly in shareholder meetings and hence in one of the most important decision-making bodies.[21] Ethical reflection on corporate

15. See www.reputationinstitute.com and also *Corporate Reputation Review*, vol. 1, no. 4, (New York 2001).

16. E.g. L.S. Cummings, "The Financial Performance of Ethical Investment Trusts: An Australian Perspective," in *Journal of Business Ethics*, vol. 25, (2000): 79-92; also G. Moore, "Corporate Social and Financial Performance: An Investigation in the U.K. Supermarket Industry," in *Journal of Business Ethics*, vol. 24, no. 3-4, (2001): 299-315.

17. E.g. M.J. King, "Sustainability: Advantaged or Disadvantaged? Do organisations that deliver value to all stakeholders produce superior financial performance?" in *The Journal of Corporate Citizenship*, Issue 3, (Autumn 2001): 99-125.

18. E. Murphy, "The Best Corporate Citizens Perform Better Financially," in *Business Ethics*, vol. 16, no. 2, (March, April 2002): 8-13.

19. L.S. Cummings, "The Financial Performance of Ethical Investment Trusts: An Australian Perspective," in *Journal of Business Ethics*, vol. 25, (2000): 79-92.

20. See www.corporatewatch.org, www.polarisinstitute.com, www.ethicalconsumer.org, www.publiccitizen.org.

21. http://ourworld.compuserve.com/homepages/critical_shareholders/

activity in an open corporate culture helps substantially to avoid unpleasant *naming and shaming* in public.

We know from research on the communication of risk that incorrect conduct in the sense of gross deviations from the expected norm is noted by people in society to a greater extent and is much more likely to be remembered than correct social behavior within the limits of legal norms.[22] What is proven for technical risks is also plausible for social and economic risks. A relativization by society's long-term memory is possible only in the long term—if at all—through countermeasures and unequivocally positive discrimination, as well as through the establishment of trusting relations. This will succeed if it can be credibly shown that the corporate activity is also in society's interest and is aimed at achieving goals which are held in high *social esteem ("shared values").*[23]

Preserving Corporate Freedom
The decision-makers in companies often complain of an excessively dense jungle of regulations with laws, directives and legal requirements. The mass of regulations in Europe is constantly being named as a reason for investments and shifting of facilities abroad; excessive regulation, according to many entrepreneurs, is jeopardizing the position of Europe as a place to do business. It is not only EU bureaucracy—so famous for defining standards for the curvature of bananas or the size of toilet seats—which suggests that such complaints are well-founded: experience shows that "less government interference" has a revitalizing effect on entrepreneurial engagement.

Companies dependent for their success on a political environment well disposed towards them, owing to a high degree of regulatory control, are in a particularly difficult position. They can only achieve long-term success on the product markets if they are viewed on the social "image markets" as legitimate actors who, as part of the solution rather than part of the problem, contribute to the common good with their activities. Image risks in this way become an integral part of the operational risks. In such a situation, legitimacy management—in the sense of striving to achieve recognition for one's actions—also becomes a prerequisite for successful marketing efforts from an ethical viewpoint.

---

22. M. Siegrist, "The influence of trust and perception of risk and benefits on the acceptance of gene technology," in *Risk Analysis*, vol. 20 (2000): 195-203.
23. T.C. Earle and G. Cvetkovich, *Social trust: Towards a cosmopolitan society* (Westport, Connecticut 1995).

However correct the criticism of excessive regulation, it has to be put into perspective by demanding an appropriate degree of responsibility: Freedom is always freedom within the constraints of responsibility, and it is thus justifiable to demand certain benefits in return at the level of ethically motivated obligations. Anyone who wants to avoid further-reaching regulation of business activities and wants to help correct misguided legal developments has to behave responsibly in a sustainable manner. Anyone who draws on the current legal situation to engage in delaying rearguard actions and defend positions which may have enjoyed the support of social consensus many years ago, but which today—and especially in the future—are perceived as illegitimate, is behaving not in an entrepreneurial but in a negligent manner.

Anyone who punishes justified criticism from within a company with bullying, instead of eliminating the factors that gave rise to the criticism, reinforces the arguments of those forces in society calling for more controls, tighter laws and thus also more government bureaucracy. There is no greater run on the television cameras and microphones by politicians than when they have a public opportunity to accuse companies of illegal or illegitimate activities and demand more controls to avoid future misdeeds.

It should also be remembered that those who take criticism of internal corporate irregularities as an opportunity to denounce and persecute critical employees, without giving any thought to how the deficits in behavioral structures came about, runs the risk that the mistakes that were made before will be made again and again.

Applied Business Ethics as Competitive Advantage
Innovation, efficiency, effectiveness, the ability to make the most of market potential and to interpret the signs of the times correctly, as well as the art of saving costs and spending at the right place and at the right time, will also retain their immense importance in the future as indispensable virtues in business. An additional element, however, will become increasingly important: The ethical quality of entrepreneurial activity. It could become a new, solid basis for future competitiveness. The greater the prosperity a society achieves, the more important immaterial values become—and the more customers there will be who take an interest in the social, ecological and political quality of the actions engaged in by the company whose goods they purchase. Recent studies estimate that about half the consumers in Denmark also want to see ethical criteria being met when they make their purchasing decisions.[24]

---

24. P. Pruzan "Corporate Reputation: Image and Identity," op. cit., 51; K. Hjulmand, *Det umuliges kunst: Politik og den politiske forbruger,* Chapter 2 (Copenhagen 1997).

At least for enlightened companies, corporate success today comprises more than simply the level of the quarterly profits. Profit making is to a company what food is to a human being—an absolute necessity. Just as no reasonable person will define his or her purpose in life as exclusively the intake of food, enlightened companies acquire legitimacy for their profit making through their social value-added. The reputation of a company is increasingly becoming one of the most valuable assets, even if it does not appear directly in the balance sheet—but this is likely to change in the very near future in view of the substantial efforts being made in the field of *social responsibility reporting*. The judgment of society which gives justification to a company's reputation depends essentially on whether that company is perceived as contributing to the implementation of social values.

Satisfaction of customer needs in the broader sense, responsible dealing with people—not only as a means to the end of higher productivity, but as an intrinsic value—as well as protection of the environment are important stones in the mosaic of "sustainable corporate success". This makes legitimate activities not only a positive end in themselves, but also represents an investment in future corporate success. A corporate culture in which the employees have internalized such a view of things is one of the most important building blocks for present and future success. This is the view moreover not only of business ethics specialists and philosophers, but also of managers in companies. They are mostly of the opinion that high standards also make good business sense ("doing well by doing good"[25]).

In all institutions around the globe, insiders know best where the strengths and weaknesses of their own organizations lie. Where critical insiders put their finger on the wounds, but cannot achieve corrective changes through normal channels and therefore leave the company (whistleblowers), it is appropriate to doubt the overall ethical climate in that organization—whichever way one looks at it, however, this kind of criticism should not serve as an opportunity for witch-hunts and stirring up images of an enemy within to be used against those who articulate their knowledge of actual or suspected deficits. Companies should regard the internal critic as a kind of internal stakeholder and cultivate "stakeholder relations" with their critics. In this way, they take advantage of a sensitive internal "early warning system" and are able to detect potential or actual problems at an earlier stage, take corrective action and aspire to "best practices" in the long term.

---

25. Katholieke Universiteit Brabant, *Management Beyond Borders. An International Study among Managers in Nine EU Countries*, (Tilburg 1996), 42f.

Indifference or even what is felt to be "clever" exploitation of ethically ambiguous practices aggravates existing problems and provokes unnecessary additional damage at the individual and corporate level, as well as the level of the common good. Concrete and sustainable efforts to work not only profitably, but also with moral impeccability raise the ethical awareness and social competence of a company. This helps to solve problems at the earliest possible juncture and at the lowest possible cost in the very places where they occur. This increases the efficiency and effectiveness of corporate activity. And that is the "Business Case" of applied business ethics.

Small Example

*Unlived life also
comes to an end
more slowly perhaps
like a battery
in a flashlight
that no one uses.
But that's of scant help
when you
(let's just say)
want to switch on
the flashlight
after so and so many years
and it gives forth
nary a glimmer
and when you open it
you find only your bones
and if you are out of luck
they too
are already eaten away.
And all that time
you could have
just as well shone.*

Erich Fried